HOW TO WIN BUSINESS
FROM THE GOVERNMENT

HOW TO WIN BUSINESS FROM THE GOVERNMENT

James J. Baker

Bartleby Press
Washington • Baltimore

Published and distributed by:

Bartleby Press
8600 Foundry Street
Savage Mill Box 2043
Savage, Maryland 20763
800-953-9929
www.BartlebythePublisher.com

ISBN: 978-0-910155-78-6

Library of Congress Control Number: 2009927953

Disclaimer: This book was written over a period of four years with the intent of helping people better understand the U.S. federal government information technology marketplace. Use of these techniques may help your company better understand the U.S. federal government marketplace but in no way guarantees your company federal contract success. The selling and research techniques discussed in this book are based on the experience of the author and his sales career spanning over the last two decades. All of the Web sites depicted in this book are from the public domain and available to anyone with access to the Internet. Please note that the government will change the location and content of a page at their discretion. The author and publisher specifically disclaim any liability that is incurred from the use or application of the contents of this book.

Printed in the United States of America

Contents

Preface

Dear Small Business Owner:

In today's market, most companies or customers don't really care about small businesses. *They only care about your value to them!* Many (not all) of the small business outreach services available to teach people about selling and marketing are done by people who are not qualified to give advice. Yes, there are many wonderful organizations with information about the government. However, there is one problem that runs through these organizations—many of the people behind the scenes, in both the public and private arenas, *have literally never closed a deal, had a sales quota, or even marketed to the federal government.*

Several years ago, I was on a panel at a big event in the D.C. Metro Area. As I met the other people on the panel, I heard them discuss what they were going to share with the audience of small business owners who had come to this seminar to learn how to market their services better. When it was my turn to speak to the panel, I asked how many of them had ever closed a deal in the federal government. After some harsh looks and eye rolling, the other panel members admitted they had never sold anything to the federal government. How amazing is this—a panel to give advice on doing business with the government and only one person (me) had ever sold anything to the feds. Unfortunately, this is not at all uncommon. There are many panels, discussions, conferences, and seminars that go on every day, handing out information that is not really useful.

At the turn of the century, I knew if I was going to exist and thrive in this market, then something had to change. So, I set out to learn the key differences between the companies (both large and small) that win in the $70 billion federal IT market and those that lose. I have had the opportunity over the last decade to interview some of the most successful business people in the marketplace as well as learn from some legendary business development people. This knowledge, coupled with the desire to share my findings with other small businesses, led to the writing of this book. Whether you are new to the government game or a seasoned pro, this book will give you insights on how to improve your approach to selling and marketing to the federal government.

The goal of this book is to teach 4 things that will help your company change how it goes after business in the federal market:

1. How to research the federal customer

2. How to build a qualified sales pipeline and execute a call plan

3. How to articulate your value proposition effectively

4. And ultimately, how to win new business

Over the last several years, I have given the "How to Win Business Seminar" to a variety of groups throughout the country. Their unanimous opinions were that this book contains excellent information in helping any technology company win new business. Some of the information in this book is a well-kept secret within the Capital Beltway that only the big guys know about. The difference between those who win and lose in the $70 billion federal information technology marketplace depends on preparation, focus, and execution.

James J. Baker, Jr.

James J. Baker, Jr.

http://www.jamesjbaker.com/
http://www.governmentbusinessbook.biz/

Finding the Low-Hanging Fruit

The goal of this book is to simply show you where to look to find out about information technology deals as well as how to access the right people and present your company in an unforgettable fashion. This will show future customers that you understand their issues and can offer them a solution to meet their requirements.

As a consultant to technology companies, I get asked the question all the time, "Where is the low-hanging fruit?" I usually respond, "I sure wish I knew." The reality is that low-hanging fruit seldom exists. Any piece of business I have ever won has been the result of tenacity, hard work, and understanding my customers' requirements. This book will literally show how to develop a sales pipeline.

In a recent focus group for this book, I asked a group of large and small business owners the key difference between those who win and those who lose in the federal information technology marketplace. I received some varied responses:

- Focusing on the right program
- Tenacity
- Patience
- Relationships
- Knocking on doors for a year and a half
- Following the money
- Getting on the right team

What all these responses have in common is, the way you win in the federal market is to be focused and prepared. So how does one get focused and prepared? *Let's begin our journey.*

Acknowledgments

This book is dedicated to the great American small businesses that keep the entrepreneurial spirit alive and kicking and make America the great country that it is.

For me, writing this book was no small task. Along the way there were many people who supported me and helped me to accomplish my goal. They deserve my special thanks.

First, however, I need to thank God, for the many wonderful prayers that he answers daily in my life.

My best friend and wife, Kelly has always believed in me and kept the fabulous Baker boys busy so I could write this book.

Steve Baldwin hired me as a newspaper salesman many years ago and then taught me the federal business. Doug Parham has imparted many lessons about life and business. I am forever grateful.

Lynne Kern did a terrific job editing this book.

Stephen Clouse showed me the secrets of an unforgettable presentation.

I can't thank my parents enough for their many lessons about the meaning of true customer service and of never giving up.

My sister Judy gave me sisterly legal advice and encouragement.

Geoff Livingston introduced me to the publisher along with his recommendation.

When I was developing this book, I created a focus group. And I am grateful for the encouragement of my many friends and business contacts who participated.

Lastly, I want to thank Jeremy Kay of Bartleby Press for publishing my book.

Chapter 1

Research

Many times over my 17 years of selling, I have been lost in the forest with no real sight of where to go and what to do next. Ultimately, it was research that shined a bright light on the dark areas of my sales and marketing plans. I cannot stress enough the importance of knowing what your customers are spending their money on, why they need information technology, and how your product or service improves their business operations. This chapter highlights the key places to research when developing your company's sales pipeline.

I have looked at the 2009 federal budget, and the government has requested approximately $70.7 billion for information technology-related goods and services. You are probably thinking, "How do I get myself some of that money?" As a company, your research should start with the government's information technology (IT) budget. By using an Internet browser and going online, we can actually see how and what the government is going to spend their money on.

Where's the Budget?

Some of the best advice I got when I started my career in selling technology to the government was *"follow the money—all agencies have it. Just pick one or two and start calling."* The best place to learn about the government's money is the President's budget. You can find the President's budget at *http://www.budget.gov* or *http://www.whitehouse .gov/omb/.* Once you are on this site, click on the link circled below, FY 2009 Budget.

Once you click on the link, a screen will come up informing you that you are leaving the White House Web server.

Next, click on the link, *http://www.gpoaccess.gov/usbudget/ browse.html* and you will come to the Government Printing Office Web page. Once on this page, click on the link circled below "George W. Bush" for the FY 2009 budget.

Next, you will come to a page that has a listing of all the departments and their budgets. I encourage you to look at the federal organization you are targeting and read all the information available about the department.

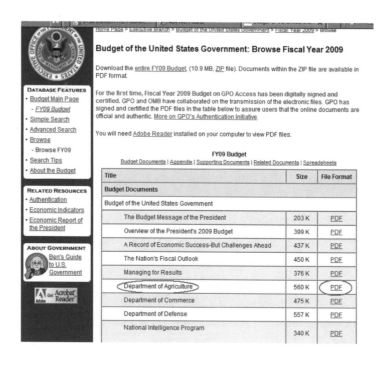

For example, if you click on the PDF link for the Department of Agriculture, you will be directed over to the Department of Agriculture's budget. This document will provide you insight into Agriculture's 2009 budget goals, programs, and spending. The following diagram is an excerpt from Agriculture's budget overview:

DEPARTMENT OF AGRICULTURE

The President's 2009 Budget will:

- Ensure the continuation of a strong farm economy and fulfill the Administration's commitment to reduce trade barriers;
- Provide nutrition assistance programs to one in five Americans;
- Maintain support for the Northwest Forest Plan by providing for the offer of 800 million board feet of timber to be harvested;
- Encourage rural development through program reforms and improved housing opportunities; and
- Help ensure the safety of both imported and domestic products.

Ensuring the Continuation of a Strong Farm Economy

After you are done reading up on the department(s) that you want to sell and market your products and services to, go back to the FY 2009 budget table at *http://www.gpoaccess.gov/usbudget/fy09/browse.html* and scroll down until you come to a section called Supplemental Materials. Click on this section and you will be directed to a table called Analytical Perspectives, Supplemental Materials. Scroll down to section 9 of the table—Integrating Services with Information Technology. This table gives you access to excellent information on E-Gov, IT programs that are on OMB's watch list, IT projects that are considered high risk, the 300's, and lines of business (LOB)—terms to be elaborated upon later in this chapter.

9. Integrating Services with Information Technology		
9-1. Effectiveness of Agency's IT Management & E-Gov Processes	104 KB	PDF
9-2. Management Guidance	71 KB	PDF
9-3. Management Watch List for FY 2008	17 KB	PDF
9-4. High Risk IT Project List As of September 30, 2007	49 KB	PDF
9-5. Agencies with IT Investments on the Management Watch List	56 KB	PDF
9-6. FY 2009 Exhibit 300 Evaluation Criteria	184 KB	PDF
9-7. Comparison of the Management Watch List by Fiscal Year	10 KB	PDF
9-8. Number of Recurring Investments on the Management Watch List	56 KB	PDF
9-9. Lines of Business (LoB) Update	36 KB	PDF
9-10. Status of E-Government Initiatives	76 KB	PDF

As you begin marketing into a new agency, it is very important to know which of its programs are having trouble and/or are at risk. Sometimes the fastest path into an agency is to have a solution for a problematic program.

Now that you have a good overview on what your target agency's budget is for 2009, it is time to take a look at the actual IT investments. Go back to the Web site *http://www.whitehouse.gov/omb/*. This time, you are going to click on Management and then click on E-Gov.

After you click on the link for E-Gov, you will have a screen that comes up on your computer that says Office of E-Government and Information Technology. Below this statement, there is a hyperlink for Visualization to Understanding Expenditures in Information Technology (VUE-IT). Click on this hyperlink and you will come to a screen that has a table of the 2009 IT spending for the federal government. Click on the link that says Download CSV Extract.

VUE-IT

(Visualization to Understand Expenditures in Information Technology)

Federal Government

Federal Government

Total Number of Investments: 6,575   FY2009 Requests: $70,716

Service Groups			Agencies		

Filters: ☐ 🔴 High Risk | ☐ 🔍 Watch List | ☐ 📋 On HR or Watch List   📊 Download CSV Extract [Download Other Lists]

Name	DME	SS	FY2009 Requests	%	Investments
Services to Citizens	$12,107	$17,571	$29,678	42%	2,291
Support Delivery of Services to Citizens	$1,204	$1,782	$2,986	4%	830
Management of Government Resources	$7,666	$25,780	$33,446	47%	3,268
Service Types and Components	$679	$3,926	$4,605	7%	186
Total	$21,657	$49,060	$70,716	100%	6,575

The CSV Extract will give you some insight on the types of technology investments the government is budgeted to buy in 2009. As you can see from the diagram below, there is going to be a considerable IT investment in supply change, knowledge, and materials management.

All dollar amounts reported in $ Millions

Federal Government

FEA Line of Business or Subfunction Mapping	Number of Investments	Total PY	Total CY	Total BY	DME PY	DME CY	DME BY	SS PY	SS CY	SS
Service Types and	2291	29732.20167	29211.8906	29678.4598	13497.0749	12609.9233	12107.077	16235.1268	16601.967	175
Federal Government	Service Group:	Services to Citizens								

FEA Line of Business or Subfunction Mapping	Number of Investments	Total PY	Total CY	Total BY	DME PY	DME CY	DME BY	SS PY	SS CY	SS
Community and Social	39	1294.102122	1254.48167	1188.43826	21.570381	15.386742	17.788093	1272.53174	1239.0949	11
Correctional Activities	6	97.9997	106.177	110.103	12.1212	6.993	5.325	85.8785	99.184	
Defense and National	268	12899.11	11685.142	11593.517	7928.804	6341.22	6003.61	4970.306	5343.922	
Disaster Management	129	495.111962	639.873413	575.09914	263.804983	360.547356	280.304393	231.306979	279.32606	29
Economic Development	64	171.583058	342.842462	281.29961	83.078448	244.640645	182.983936	88.50461	98.201817	99
Education	137	567.342	582.335688	591.473	51.124	63.023596	53.565	516.218	519.31209	
Energy	54	73.426734	77.803097	70.768904	15.205527	24.584768	13.587448	58.223207	53.218309	5
Environmental	173	796.973633	788.721694	860.347103	179.6127	173.407652	244.54	617.360933	615.31404	61
General Science and	218	937.44257	992.362027	960.160987	298.78622	297.498585	284.892436	638.65635	694.86344	679
Health	494	5204.438	5060.49517	5398.30662	1323.133	1256.27117	1404.33562	3881.305	3604.214	
Homeland Security	135	2046.655922	2474.08951	2551.18777	1006.57015	1499.80052	1185.7956	1040.08577	974.28899	136
Income Security	34	563.349287	522.408121	591.260351	184.546414	163.962799	182.7333	378.802873	358.44532	408
Intelligence Operations	40	419.11	489.964	471.276	167.719	254.871	166.7	251.391	235.093	
International Affairs and Commerce	33	76.6912	81.84884	69.50925	37.5837	36.0286	16.2659	39.1075	45.82024	53
Law Enforcement	89	751.156717	772.695354	833.652199	320.816717	327.61266	356.195079	430.34	445.08269	
Litigation and Judicial	33	67.407423	58.948167	66.063146	29.828	20.25	21.657	37.579423	38.698167	44
Natural Resources	120	226.654087	225.94449	230.870739	39.72957	32.883153	30.406	186.924517	193.06134	20
Transportation	183	2926.428519	2950.45287	3128.1531	1498.71885	1450.008	1619.0922	1427.70967	1500.4449	1
Workforce Management	42	117.216739	105.315	106.9736	34.322	40.933	37.3	82.894739	64.382	
total for Service Types and Components	2291	29732.20167	29211.8906	29678.4598	13497.0749	12609.9233	12107.077	16235.1268	16601.967	17

By the time this book goes to press, the Obama Administration will still be in first 100 days of office. I encourage you to go back to the VUE-IT Web site to learn more about the government's investment in information technology. President Obama and Vice President Biden have made their technology plans for government very clear. I encourage you to visit *http://www.whitehouse.gov/agenda/technology/*, where you can learn more about the following technology goals:

- Safeguarding and strengthening the digital environment

- Protecting the openness of the Internet

- Government accountability / transparency

- Hiring a national CTO

- Deploying next generation broadband

- Reforming the patent system

- Investing in electronic health care information systems

As we all prepare for the new era in government, I also encourage you to view some of the information on the Technology, Innovation and Government Reform (TIGR) team at *http://change.gov/newsroom/entry/inside_the_transition_technology_innovation_and_government_reform/*. There is a very interesting video they posted about technology and government the day before the inauguration, as indicated in the following diagram.

Inside the Transition: Technology, Innovation and Government Reform

Monday, January 19, 2009 02:30pm EST / Posted by Kate Albright-Hanna

The Obama Administration's commitment to reform and transparency is embodied by the one of the Transition's most dynamic groups—the TIGR (Technology, Innovation and Government Reform) Team.

The experts who serve in TIGR advocated for some of our most innovative features on Change.gov —including the Citizen's Briefing Book and Seat at the Table. Watch the video and get to know the people behind the ideas—and let us know your reaction to some of the initiatives they're proposing.

Let's not forget W...

I updated this section of the book just a few days after President Obama's inauguration. As President Obama and his cabinet set out on their course to change government, I want to spend a little time reflecting on how the Bush Administration reported spending on information technology. As the new administration impacts government spending, many of the current budgets and technology plans impacting government were conceived under the Bush Administration. It is therefore very important to understand how Bush communicated the budget to the public. My opinion is that Obama will build off of some of the excellent changes Bush made happen in IT spending. As I mentioned earlier in this chapter, the federal budget, as far back as I can remember, has always been posted at *http://www.whitehouse.gov/omb/ budget/fy2009/. Under the Bush Administration, one could access the Report for IT Spending at the above referenced Web site. This report was a 6,000 plus line item budget description of all the IT spending.* The Obama Administration has currently taken down the budget *Report for IT Spending.* President Obama has a statement on the budget Web site that a new Office for E-Government and IT Spending Web site is coming soon. I am assuming that President Obama's Administration will report IT spending in a similar fashion. As of the last week of January 2009, President Obama has not updated any of the new budget sites with a detailed breakdown of information technology spending. Generally, budget updates will happen in February of 2009. With that being said, I will post all budget updates on my Web site, *http://www.governmentbusinessbook.biz/.*

Now, let's go back eight years ago to some of the new changes that were implemented in government by the Bush Administration. The Quick Silver Initiatives were changing the way the government and industry did business. I encourage you to spend some time looking at President Bush's Management Agenda from 2002. In short, the Quick Silver Initiatives were the Bush Administration's plan to improve the business of government to the citizen as well as other federal departments.

The *Report on IT Spending* was a spreadsheet that listed the IT budget for each department of the federal government. The report provided you information about the project, the line of business it supported, and current funding, as shown in the following diagram.

Investment Title	Investment Description (limited to 255 characters)	Total Investments ($M)			Primary FEA Mapping (BRM or SRM)		Development/Modernization/ Enhancement ($M)		
		FY2007	FY2008	FY2009	FY2007	FY2008	FY2009	FY2007	FY2008
Defense Enterprise Accounting and Management System-Air Force	DEAMS AF initiative drives improved information technology management, enabling integration of all financial information to produce accurate and timely financial statements, and the ability for accurate budget forecasting.	$20.6	$26.6	$60.0	402	124	$12.4	$23.4	$59.0

There were over six thousand budget lines on this report just for 2009. Since the report was made in Microsoft Excel, anyone could do a keyword search by hitting Ctrl+F, and a search window would appear enabling you to search through the budget by typing a keyword.

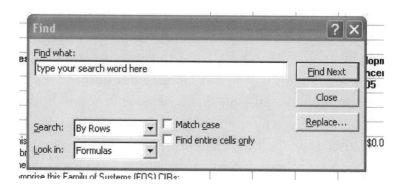

For example, if you are interested in selling security solutions to the government, you could do a keyword search on security. Chances are the government is buying what you are selling. After typing in a keyword and clicking Find Next, you would automatically be taken to sections of the spreadsheet where the keyword is mentioned.

As the Bush Administration comes to an end and the Obama Administration begins, there are some important budget terms you need to familiarize yourself with:

- Steady State

- Development, Modernization, and Enhancement (DME)

- Total Investments

- Line of Business (LOB)

Steady State refers to maintenance and operation funding that is already allocated to a program to maintain the program's current capability and performance level. In the following chart I have circled where you can look to find the Steady State funding for the Obama Administration.

All dollar amounts reported in $ Millions										
Federal Government										
FEA Line of Business or Subfunction	Number of Investment	Total PY	Total CY	Total BY	DME PY	DME CY	DME BY	SS PY	SS CY	SS BY
Service Types and Components	2291	29732.2	29211.89	29678.46	13497.07	12609.92	12107.08	16295.13	16601.97	17571.38
Federal Government	Service Group:	Services to Citizens								
FEA Line of Business or Subfunction	Number of Investment	Total PY	Total CY	Total BY	DME PY	DME CY	DME BY	SS PY	SS CY	SS BY
Community and Social Services	39	1294.102	1254.482	1188.438	21.57038	15.38674	17.78809	1272.532	1239.095	1170.65
Correctional Activities	6	97.9997	106.177	110.103	12.1212	6.993	5.325	85.8785	99.184	104.778
Defense and National Security	268	12899.11	11685.14	11593.52	7928.804	6341.22	6003.61	4970.306	5343.922	5589.907
Disaster Management	129	495.112	639.8734	575.0991	263.805	360.5474	280.3044	231.307	279.3261	294.7947
Economic Development	64	171.5831	342.8425	281.2996	83.07845	244.6406	182.9839	88.50461	98.20182	98.31567
Education	137	567.342	582.3357	591.473	51.124	63.0236	53.565	516.218	519.3121	537.908
Energy	54	73.42873	77.8031	70.7689	15.20553	24.58479	13.58745	58.22321	53.21831	57.18146
Environmental Management	173	796.9736	788.7217	860.3471	179.6127	173.4077	244.54	617.3609	615.314	615.8071
General Science and Innovation	218	937.4426	992.362	960.161	298.7862	297.4986	284.8924	638.6564	694.8634	675.2686
Health	494	5204.438	5060.485	5398.307	1323.133	1256.271	1404.336	3881.305	3804.214	3993.971
Homeland Security	135	2046.656	2474.09	2551.188	1006.57	1499.801	1185.796	1040.086	974.289	1365.392
Income Security	34	563.3493	522.4081	591.2604	184.5464	163.9628	182.7333	378.8029	358.4453	408.5271
Intelligence Operations	40	419.11	489.964	471.276	167.719	254.871	166.7	251.391	235.093	304.576
International Affairs and Commerce	33	76.6912	81.84884	69.50925	37.5837	36.0286	16.2659	39.1075	45.82024	53.24335
Law Enforcement	89	751.1567	772.6954	833.6522	320.8167	327.6127	356.1951	430.34	445.0827	477.4571
Litigation and Judicial Activities	33	67.40742	58.94817	66.06315	29.828	20.25	21.657	37.57942	38.69817	44.40615
Natural Resources	120	226.6541	225.9445	230.8707	39.72957	32.88315	30.406	186.9245	193.0613	200.4647
Transportation	183	2926.429	2950.453	3128.153	1498.719	1450.008	1619.092	1427.71	1500.445	1509.061
Workforce Management	42	117.2167	105.315	106.9736	34.322	40.933	37.3	82.89474	64.382	69.6736
total for Service Types and Componer	2291	29732.2	29211.89	29678.46	13497.07	12609.92	12107.08	16235.13	16601.97	17571.38

The following graphic is a budget line item from Bush's 2009 *Report on IT Spending*. Steady State is circled.

Investment Title	Investment Description (limited to 255 characters)	Total Investments ($M)			Primary FEA Mapping (BRM or SRM)		Development/Modernization/ Enhancement ($M)			Steady State ($M)		
		FY2007	FY2008	FY2009	FY2007	FY2008	FY2009	FY2007	FY2008	FY2009	FY2007	FY2008
Defense Enterprise Accounting and Management System–Air Force	DEAMS AF initiative drives improved information technology management, enabling integration of all financial information to produce accurate and timely financial statements, and the ability for accurate budget forecasting.	$20.6	$26.6	$60.0	402	124	$12.4	$23.4	$59.0	$8.2	$3.2	$1.0

Development, Modernization, and Enhancement (DME) refers to new money that is going into a program. In the diagram below I have circled where you can look for information on DME funding under the Obama Administration. Remember this is new money for a program.

All dollar amounts reported in $ Millions										
Federal Government										
FEA Line of Business or Subfunction Mapping	Number of Investments	Total PY	Total CY	Total BY	DME PY	DME CY	DME BY	SS PY	SS CY	SS BY
Service Types and Components	2291	29732.2	29211.89	29678.46	13497.67	12609.92	12407.08	16235.13	16601.97	1757
						↓				
Federal Government	Service Group:	Services to Citizens			DME Funding					
FEA Line of Business or Subfunction Mapping	Number of Investments	Total PY	Total CY	Total BY	DME PY	DME CY	DME BY	SS PY	SS CY	SS BY
Community and Social Services	39	1294.102	1254.482	1188.438	21.57038	15.38674	17.78809	1272.532	1239.095	1170
Correctional Activities	6	97.9997	106.177	110.103	12.1212	6.993	5.325	85.8785	99.184	104.7
Defense and National Security	268	12899.11	11685.14	11593.52	7928.804	6341.22	6003.61	4970.306	5343.922	5589.9

In the following chart from Bush's 2009 *Report on IT Spending*, I have circled the DME funding category.

Investment Title	Investment Description (limited to 255 characters)	Total Investments ($M)			Primary FEA Mapping (BRM or SRM)		Development/Modernization/ Enhancement ($M)			Steady State ($M)		
		FY2007	FY2008	FY2009	FY2007	FY2008	FY2009	FY2007	FY2008	FY2003	FY2007	FY2008
Defense Enterprise Accounting and Management System- Air Force	DEAMS AF initiative drives improved information technology management, enabling integration of all financial information to produce accurate and timely financial statements, and the ability for accurate budget forecasting.	$20.6	$26.6	$60.0	402	124	$12.4	$23.4	$59.0	$8.2	$3.2	$1.0

This program is going to get $59 million in DME funding in 2009. Overall, the government will spend a total of $60 million in 2009: $1 million in Steady State and $59 million in new funding. **Total Investments** are the sum of Steady State and DME funding. When President Obama releases the updated budget information later this year, you should look for programs whose modernization funding matches their total investments. You will only find a handful of these programs but these are the "diamonds in the rough" because these are brand-spanking-new programs without an incumbent. These are the best targets to chase.

In 2004, the Office of Management and Budget (OMB) created **Lines of Business (LOB)** to help the government find ways to save money by using common cross-agency processes. The theory behind LOBs is, if something works for one agency, maybe it could work for another.

There are currently nine LOBs:

- Financial Management (FM)
- Human Resources (HR)
- Grants Management (GM)

- Case Management (CM)

- Federal Health Architecture (FHA)

- Information Systems Security (ISS)

- Budget Formulation and Execution (BFE)

- Geospatial

- IT Infrastructure (ITI)

"Baker, why should I care about LOBs?"

All LOBs have some aspect of information technology as a major or subcomponent. If we can help one agency save money in a particular LOB, we can look every government person managing any LOB in the eye and tell them about the LOB success agency XYZ experienced using our product or service. In my opinion, the established LOBs will be a good starting point for the new national CTO to study how government is currently working to become more efficient in managing technology resources.

I recently read an article where IBM was added to the GSA HR LOB approved vendors list. I can think of a couple ways to market being on an approved GSA LOB vendors list.

To learn more about LOBs, please visit *http://www.gpoaccess .gov/usbudget/fy09/spec.html* and click on the PDF file in section 9 on LOB, as circled in the following graphic.

9. Integrating Services with Information Technology		
9-1. Effectiveness of Agency's IT Management & E-Gov Processes	104 KB	PDF
9-2. Management Guidance	71 KB	PDF
9-3. Management Watch List for FY 2008	17 KB	PDF
9-4. High Risk IT Project List As of September 30, 2007	49 KB	PDF
9-5. Agencies with IT Investments on the Management Watch List	56 KB	PDF
9-6. FY 2009 Exhibit 300 Evaluation Criteria	184 KB	PDF
9-7. Comparison of the Management Watch List by Fiscal Year	10 KB	PDF
9-8. Number of Recurring Investments on the Management Watch List	56 KB	PDF
9-9. Lines of Business (LoB) Update	36 KB	PDF
9-10. Status of E-Government Initiatives	76 KB	PDF

As we await President Obama's updates to the IT budget, I want to take a look at how the Bush Administration represented the LOB in the *Report on IT Spending*. In the following spreadsheet, I have circled the section of the budget that indicates the agency's LOB.

Investment Title	Investment Description (limited to 255 characters)	Total Investments ($M)			Primary FEA Mapping (BRM or SRM)		Development/Modernization/ Enhancement ($M)		
		FY2007	FY2008	FY2009	FY2007	FY2008	FY2009	FY2007	FY2008
Defense Enterprise Accounting and Management System-Air Force	DEAMS AF initiative drives improved information technology management, enabling integration of all financial information to produce accurate and timely financial statements, and the ability for accurate budget forecasting.	$20.6	$26.6	$60.0	402	124	$12.4	$23.4	$59.0

Below the Primary FEA Mapping section, the number 402 is listed in the left column. This means there is a Financial

Management (FM) subcomponent to this budget line item. The number in the right column refers to the sub-function of service component, in this case, the number is 124. This number refers to accounting. As professionals who sell to the federal government, we should commit all the subcomponents and sub-functions to memory—just kidding. There is an easy way to find out what this information means. I usually call OMB directly and ask questions. I find communication with actual people is generally more helpful and insightful than reading through volumes of Web pages. I have circled the number for OMB in the diagram below. You can access great contact information on OMB by going to *http://www.whitehouse.gov/omb/gils/gil-circ.aspx.*

AGENCY PROGRAM: OMB assists the President in overseeing the preparation of the Federal budget and in supervising its administration in Federal agencies. It also oversees and coordinates the Administration's procurement, financial management, information, and regulatory policies. OMB's system of Circulars and Bulletins is integral to carrying out these responsibilities.

AVAILABLILITY:
    Distributor Name: WWW Server
    Organization: Office of Management and Budget
    URL Address: http://www.whitehouse.gov/omb
    Order Process: Circulars and selected Bulletins are available on the Internet. Users can either access OMB's home page directly using the URL cited above or by going through the White House web server: http://www.whitehouse.gov
    Available Linkage Type: Text/plain; selected PDF.

ACCESS CONSTRAINTS: None
USE CONSTRAINTS: None

POINT OF CONTACT FOR FURTHER INFORMATION:
    Name: Administration Office
    Organization: Office of Management and Budget
    Street Address: 725 17th Street, NW
    City: Washington
    State: DC
    Zip Code: 20503
    Country: USA
    Network Address: N/A
    Hours of Service: 9:00 a.m. - 5:00 p.m., Monday through Friday
    Telephone: (202) 395-3080

After speaking with OMB, I recommend printing a copy of the "E-Gov Federal Enterprise Architecture Reference Model Mapping Quick Guide." This guide contains a listing of all the LOB service and sub-function codes. Understanding the LOB will help us tailor our sales and technology approach to the opportunity. More information can be found on the types of LOBs at the following link: *http://www.whitehouse.gov/omb/e-gov/fea/*.

Home > Management > E-Gov

Federal Enterprise Architecture (FEA)

Got questions? Send email to fea@omb.eop.gov

Guidance

- Federal Segment Architecture Methodology (FSAM) (FSAM website)
- Consolidated Federal Segment Architecture Methodology (CIO Council website)
- FEA Practice Guidance (PDF, 1,639kb)
- Practical Guide to Federal Service Oriented Architecture (CIO Council website)

FEA Reference Models

- Consolidated Reference Model Version 2.3 (PDF, 655kb)
- Consolidated Reference Model - Download XML (XML, 444kb)
- FY10 FEA Reference Model Mapping Quick Guide (PDF, 322kb)

When preparing to call a senior government executive, a great deal can be learned from these numbers, such as:

- Agency's mission area
- Bureau that gets funding

• Is it a major or non-major investment?

Before we move on, I again want to emphasize there were over 6,900 line items for the 2009 budget. Our best bet is to focus on only one or two agencies. For example, the Environmental Protection Agency (EPA) for 2009 has over 160 budget line items and the Treasury has over 300 budget line items. There is no easy way to do this. *You must take the time to read through each budget line item concerning the agency or agencies on which you decide to focus, and start looking at potential deals in advance.* This will be an invaluable exercise for both salespeople and senior management, since it will provide a true sense of where the money is. I teach this technique in many of my seminars; this type of analyzing is a new way of finding business for many of the attendees. *Again, stop and think* about what I am saying here. The government is telling us what technology programs get Steady State and new money as well as what they are looking to buy. This is an excellent place to start fishing in the big federal pond.

For Department of Defense (DoD) budgets, I also recommend going to this Web site:
https://snap.pae.osd.mil/snapit/BudgetDocs2009.aspx/.

This Web site is an excellent resource to learn about DoD Enterprise Information Environment Mission Area (EIEMA), government budget training documents, and specific DoD program overviews. Here is a sample of one of the Power-Point slides I downloaded:

As we can see from the preceding diagram, this Web site is full of valuable information about each DoD customer. We can also learn about select capital investments on DoD programs. I would never make a call to a senior defense executive without doing my homework first. Take a look at the following diagrams that I was able to look at by clicking on the *Select Capital Investment Report.*

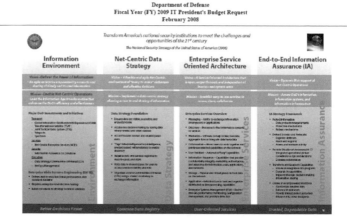

By reading this report, we can learn the following:

- A summary and justification for the budget
- Capital Planning Investment Control (CPIC)
- Spending break down of program over multiple years
- Program highlights and milestones
- Government people managing the program

- Contractors who are working on the project and what they are doing

- Who the government's customers are for this program

This report provides some very useful information about what the government is doing, how they are spending the American taxpayers' money, and the key goals of their programs.

When making calls to senior government decision-makers, having a clear understanding of their key issues is a surefire way to get a face-to-face meeting with them and another opportunity to talk about your company. One of the biggest complaints I hear from government managers is that industry does not understand their current business challenges.

Technology Strategy

Looking at the budget gives us an idea of which agencies are buying what we are selling. Once we have chosen our target agencies, I recommend looking at each agency's mission statement and goals. Look for the programs that support their goals. We can find most of this out by simply looking at each agency's Web site. I specialize in helping companies sell into the $70 billion federal technology marketplace. Yet, I always print a copy of our target agency's strategy and goals. Let's take the Internal Revenue Service (IRS) for example. Go to the Web site *http://www.treasury.gov/* and type the word *technology* in the search box. The following Web page should appear on your computer screen.

Next, click on the link that says U.S. Treasury Office of the CIO (OCIO). If you click on the About Treasury link in the menu on the left of the screen, it takes you to a link for their strategic plan. This is a great asset to have when making a sales call. In the preceding diagram, the arrows indicate your major focus points—read this information in detail.

The biggest complaint I hear from the many government executives I speak with is that industry does not know enough about their business. I have heard many federal executives say they do not look forward to a PowerPoint presentation on how great someone's technology company is. *What senior federal executives want to know is how you really help them solve their problems.* One of the best places to learn about an agency's problems is in their strategic plan, which is usually located on the agency's Web site.

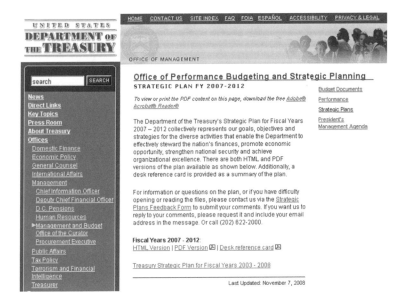

After you read the strategic plan, I encourage you to review all the information on the CIO's Web page. You can learn valuable information on the CIO page, such as:

- Mission of Agency

- Key Personnel

- OCIO Programs

In Chapter 5, Communicating Your Value Proposition, we will discuss a technique that will help you make the best presentation ever.

What the government wants to hear?

Several years ago in Atlanta, Georgia, I taught my "How to Win Business in the Federal Government Seminar" for a group of Federal Aviation Administration (FAA) employees. After finishing my hour-long presentation, I opened the floor for questions or comments. I answered a few questions on selling and research before a gray-haired woman stood up and said: "I have a comment to make."

She explained that she was a federal employee auditing my course on behalf of the government. I immediately thought, "Oh no, here comes the hammer!" However, this very nice woman went on to say that if industry would spend the proper time preparing to speak with them, using their words, and clearly understand their issues, then industry would be far more effective in marketing and selling their technology products and services.

Many technology firms will communicate with a government customer by saying, "I am company XYZ and we are a small, woman-owned, 8(a), veteran-owned, Native American firm that does IT stuff. Please buy from me?" This now wonderful, wise woman finished by telling my audience, "Listen to this young man, he knows what he is talking about."

Remember, your sales and marketing messages should always be about the government customer and their challenges!

Reading the customer's strategic plan and mission goals is the best way to learn their issues and language. Here is the Treasury's strategic plan:

Table of Contents

This strategic plan provides detailed information about how the agency works and thinks. Remember, many agencies are the size of GM or Ford. They are the equivalent of huge Fortune 500 companies with many complex layers and issues. Take the time to know the customer!

SADBU / OSDBU Forecast

Each year the government sets small business goals. All Small and Disadvantaged Business Utilization (SADBU) and Office of Small and Disadvantaged Business Utilization (OSDBU) branches post a small business forecast on their Web sites. The small business program was created to give small businesses a fair chance at competing for federal procurements. If a large contractor wants federal dollars, then that company has to show they have been giving a certain percentage to small and/or disadvantaged businesses. When speaking with a SADBU or OSDBU, take their advice with a grain of salt. With respect to some of the many wonderful SADBU and OSBDUs I have encountered over the years at the FAA and Department of Homeland Security (DHS), they are not equipped to help small businesses *win* business—they can only provide guidance and general information about the agency, including points of contact. Most SADBU and OSBDU personnel have never worked in a 30-60-90 sales environment or have had to forecast a sales pipeline; they have never closed a deal in the federal government.

In my opinion, SADBU and OSDBUs are not business development experts or salespeople. The best place to get advice on how to sell in the government is from people who have successfully sold in the marketplace. My goal when speaking with SADBU or OSDBU is to merely get recommendations. *Let me make it clear that my statements are not meant to disparage the small business program and the good folks who support it.* Remember SADBU or OSDBUs best service is their knowledge of contacts in an agency. The following is a sample of an OSDBU Web page that contains a link to a forecast.

Procurement Opportunity Search by Category

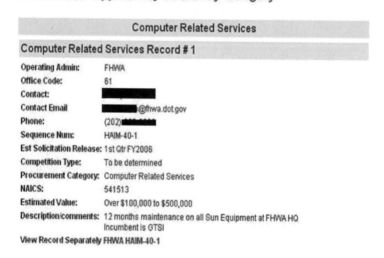

	Computer Related Services

Computer Related Services Record # 1

Operating Admin:	FHWA
Office Code:	61
Contact:	███████
Contact Email	███████@fhwa.dot.gov
Phone:	(202)███████
Sequence Num:	HAIM-40-1
Est Solicitation Release:	1st Qtr FY2006
Competition Type:	To be determined
Procurement Category:	Computer Related Services
NAICS:	541513
Estimated Value:	Over $100,000 to $500,000
Description/comments:	12 months maintenance on all Sun Equipment at FHWA HQ Incumbent is GTSI
View Record Separately	FHWA HAIM-40-1

I was researching a Federal Highway Administration deal for a client of mine at the time. Some important questions to ask when calling about an opportunity are:

1. Will this be coming up for recompete?

2. Is the opportunity in the budget? (You know how to look up the budget now!) Is there funding to support this program? Does it have DME or Steady State funding?

3. Is it funded by Congress?

4. Who is the incumbent?

5. Who are the government managers and executives involved on both the contracts side of the house and on the technical side of the house?

6. Is there a business case for this opportunity I may read?

7. How did the Program Assessment Rating Tool (PART), discussed later in this chapter, rate this program?

8. What problem is the agency trying to solve?

Take a look at all the small business deals in your targeted agencies and add them to your forecast. But remember, unless a deal can be tracked back to a budget line item, it may not be funded. *Only pursue deals with funding. I repeat, only pursue deals with funding!* I have seen too many people get fired for chasing a deal that has no money. Trust me, people can forecast until the cows come home that a deal is getting funded, but a forecast is not approval by Congress to fund a program.

Business Cases & 300's

In 1996, the *Clinger-Cohen Act* (CCA) was passed. It stated that all major agency technology purchases must go through a review board.

I encourage spending some time at the Library of Congress (*http://www.loc.gov/*) and the OMB (*http://www.omb.gov/*) Web sites to read up on this important legislation, which has had a profound impact on the way we sell and market to the government.

Essentially, the CCA consists of the *Information Technology Management Reform Act of 1996* and the *Federal Acquisition Reform Act of 1996*. The CCA was designed to simplify the way the federal government buys IT services and products. The CCA requires each agency and their individual programs to establish performance-based management principles as well as establish a chief information officer.

The Clinton and Gore era of the '90s truly changed government. Many of the government contract shops were getting eliminated or downsized, and the idea of using the GSA and Government-wide Acquisition Contract (GWAC) was gaining popularity.

The incoming Bush Administration continued to enforce agencies justifying their funding through the business case. Before any agency makes a purchase, the Investment Review Board (IRB) of that specific agency should review the program. 300 A is the business case form an agency must fill out to get money from Congress.

When deciding to market to an agency, find out the agency's specific business cases. Know the customer's business case before approaching a senior government manager or director. Here is a snapshot of some of the key information the government publishes in a business case.

Part 1: Acquisition Background and Objectives	
Topic	**Information Requested**
Date of the Acquisition Plan	This same date should also be entered in Exhibit 300, Section I.G. Acquisition Strategy
Name of Project	Provide the name of the project on the Exhibit 300.
Title of Acquisition	Provide a short descriptive title of the acquisition.
Statement of Need	Briefly describe the purpose of the acquisition, including the delivery of products and/or services.
Background	Describe the contractual history of the project and this specific acquisition.
Estimated Cost	Provide the total estimated cost and duration, including any options or phases, of the acquisition. Provide the rationale supporting the estimated costs.
Alternatives Analysis	Describe the alternative solutions you considered for accomplishing the purpose of this acquisition. Describe the results of your analysis of the feasibility/performance/benefits and cost for each alternative. Identify the costs for each alternative, how those costs were derived and the date of your analysis. Identify the selected alternative and the reasons for the selection. (Note: The FAIR Act and OMB Circular A-76 considerations should be separately addressed below.)
Risk Mitigation Strategy	Identify technical, cost and schedule risks that may affect the acquisition. What efforts are planned or underway to reduce those risks?
Funding	Describe how the funding will be obtained for this acquisition and the schedule for obtaining adequate funds at the time they are required.
Acquisition Team	Identify the acquisition team members and each member's role in the acquisition.

Some agencies make it easy to access their business cases; they make them available on their Web site and easy to download. Other agencies will not give them out. To get these business cases, you have to make a *Freedom of Information Act* (FOIA) request. There are also independent companies out there that will go and get the business cases for you. I highly recommend Jim Kerrigan of COLMAR Corporation, who does a wonderful job getting all the available business cases.

In fact, I just wrapped up two full days of looking at 101 business cases posted by DHS. All agencies are different in how they display and have you access business cases. DHS posts their business cases at the following Web site: *http://www.dhs.gov/xabout/budget/.* When visiting this Web site, you will literally see a screen where DHS contains all of its published business cases.

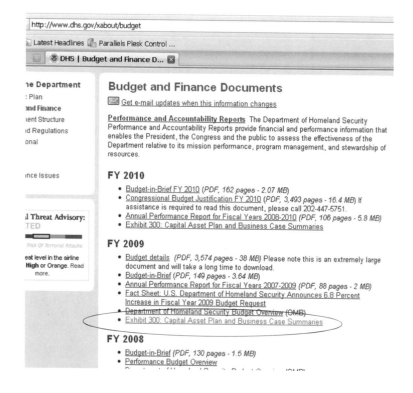

By gaining access to a business case, we can learn some truly wonderful information about our sales prospect. Let's take a moment to look at DHS business cases for the Homeland Secure Data Network (HSDN). Most DHS business cases are four pages long and are packed with some really valuable information. First read the program description.

DHS Exhibit 300 Public Release BY09 (Form) **/ A&O - Homeland Security Information Network (HSIN) (2009)** (Item)

Form Report, printed by: Administrator, System, **Feb 6, 2008**

OVERVIEW

General Information	
1. Date of Submission:	Sep 5, 2007
2. Agency:	Department of Homeland Security
3. Bureau:	Management
4. Name of this Capital Asset:	A&O - Homeland Security Information Network (HSIN) (2009)
5. Unique ID:	024-10-01-06-01-9102-00
(For IT investments only, see section 53. For all other, use agency ID system.)	

All investments

6. What kind of investment will this be in FY2009?
(Please NOTE: Investments moving to O&M ONLY in FY2009, with Planning/Acquisition activities prior to FY2009 should not select O&M. These investments should indicate their current status.)
Mixed Life Cycle

7. What was the first budget year this investment was submitted to OMB?
FY2004

8. Provide a brief summary and justification for this investment, including a brief description of how this closes in part or in whole an identified agency performance gap. [LIMIT: 2500 char]
The DHS Homeland Security Information Network (HSIN) develops and operates the primary DHS conduit through which information on domestic terrorist threats and incident management is shared at all levels. Its principal function is to provide the means for information and Sensitive But Unclassified (SBU) intelligence dissemination. HSIN provides the core services of the DHS National Operations Center (NOC) mission-specific applications, including hosting the Common Operating Picture (COP) and its analytic tools. HSIN is the primary National information sharing and collaboration tool in responding to the information sharing needs of all DHS Components Operations and stakeholder users. HSIN facilitates the gathering, assessing and analyzing of information to maintain authoritative situational awareness through the use of user-created "Virtual Situation Rooms" on the network where online conversations may be held in real-time by a number of relevant users.

Next, find out what percentage of the investment will be for hardware, software, and services. The following screenshot shows that 52 percent of the 2009 funding will be of interest to your company if you are in the services business.

Area	Percentage
Hardware	29.64
Software	1.03
Services	52.02
Other	17.31
Total	100.00

After reading the program description and percentage breakdown, look at the funding breakdown. DHS breaks down their funding information into three categories: past year (PY), current year (CY), and budget year (BY). Remember, these numbers are given in millions.

	PY-1 & Earlier	PY	CY	BY
	2006	2007	2008	2009
Planning:				
Budgetary Resources	0.000	0.000	0.000	0.000
Acquisition:				
Budgetary Resources	68.300	0.000	0.000	0.000
TOTAL, sum of stages:				
Budgetary Resources	68.300	0.000	0.000	0.000
Maintenance:				
Budgetary Resources	43.999	32.654	33.100	47.673
TOTAL, All Stages				
Budgetary Resources	112.299	32.654	33.100	47.673
Government FTE Costs	0.000	0.000	0.000	0.000
# of FTEs	0.00	0.00	0.00	0.00
Total, BR + FTE Cost	112.299	32.654	33.100	47.673

What makes federal selling great is how open the government is and how much can be learned. I realize there are stories about the government buying $100 toilet seats and hammers, *but make no mistake friend, the government is a very, very smart buyer.* As a sales or marketing person, these business cases are pure gold. Use them to learn the customer's issues and how to give tailor-made solutions that meet their requirements.

Program Assessment Rating Tool (PART)

The Program Assessment Rating Tool (PART) tells us whether or not an agency is doing a good job with its program. The government has a great system that monitors which programs are doing well and which are doing poorly. This book will only scratch the top of the Capital Planning Investment Control (CPIC) process. CPIC is an approach many agencies use to plan their IT investments. I recommend checking out the Google U.S. Government Search portal (*http://www. google .com/unclesam*) to learn how the government plans its IT investments—they generally plan a year to a year and half in advance. To learn more about PART, take a look at the ExpectMore Web site at *http://www.expectmore.gov/*.

As you become more familiar with the way the government operates, you will be able to tailor your communications to government. Let's say a federal agency wants to spend taxpayer dollars on a certain need. The agency has to fill out Form 300 A, which tells Congress their business reasons for this expenditure. If the business case is approved, then Congress will appropriate funding for this program. Looking at the 53's of an agency helps when making a true determination of what type of programs are getting funded.

There is some confusion concerning the difference between a 53 and what actually goes into the budget. During the writing of this book, I placed several calls to OMB as well as the E-Gov office and have received varied responses. Essentially, the 53 is an IT investment portfolio that agencies send to OMB for their budget funding. An overview of each agency's budget is provided at this Web site: *http://www.whitehouse.gov/omb/*.

A budget narrative

Let me provide a little history of the budget and how it works. The *Budget and Accounting Act of 1921* states that the President must submit a budget to Congress on or after the first Monday in January but no later than the first Monday in February. I generally find the government to be a pretty quite place from Christmas time through Dr. King's birthday. The budget is usually sent to Congress on the first Monday in February, giving Congress almost 8 months to review the budget before the next fiscal year begins. The goal of this book is to help you sell to the federal government. To explain in detail how the total budget process works would require several more chapters. The important thing to know is that government agencies can only spend what Congress has appropriated. However, I really encourage reading up on how the budget process works. For information on the budget process, refer to this Web site: *http://www.gpoaccess.gov/usbudget/fy09/browse.html*. In the following graphic, circled is a report that provides additional information on the federal budget.

Analytical Perspectives	2.9 MB	PDF
Supplemental Materials		
Historical Tables	2.5 MB	PDF
Appendix		
Mid-Session Review for FY 2009	1.4 MB	PDF
Supporting Documents		
Major Savings and Reforms in the President's 2009 Budget	1.17 MB	PDF
Federal Credit Supplement	627 K	PDF
Object Class Analysis	958 K	PDF
Balances of Budget Authority	933 K	PDF
Budget System and Concepts	271 K	PDF
Budget Amendments and Supplementals		

The OMB helps the President make the budget by getting budget data from agencies and compiling it into the final budget to be approved by the President. Keep in mind that the totals for the budget are only projected amounts of what an agency needs. Once the President submits the budget, Congress then has to approve the amount. It is very important to check if a program has truly received funding.

The government works on a fiscal year that starts on October 1st and ends on September 30th. Generally, the President will send the budget to Congress at least 18 months before the fiscal year begins. This is why when a deal hits the street, you really should be tracking it well in advance. Remember, the 53 is what an agency submits for budget requests to OMB. Understanding what is on an agency's 53 is very important in marketing and selling to the government.

"Wait a minute, Baker!"

You may be thinking, "I thought you said all I have to do is go to the OMB Web site and look at the budget." Yes, you do need to visit the OMB Web site, but there is a difference between what is forecasted in the budget and what actually *gets approved*.

The ExpectMore Web site gives you an overview of which federal programs are doing well and which ones are having a tougher time. Here is what the ExpectMore Web site looks like:

When I start looking at an agency's PART ratings, I generally look at Results Not Demonstrated programs. The Results Not Demonstrated feature can have 2 meanings:

1. The program is not doing well and may not get future funding

2. This is an opportunity to help the government fix a problem

Department of Agriculture	Conservation Technical Assistance	Results Not Demonstrated
Department of Agriculture	Dairy Payment Program	Results Not Demonstrated
Department of Agriculture	Dairy Price Support Program	Results Not Demonstrated
Department of Agriculture	Emergency Watershed Protection Program	Results Not Demonstrated
Department of Agriculture	Food and Nutrition Service - Child and Adult Care Food Program	Results Not Demonstrated
Department of Agriculture	Forest Service: Invasive Species Program	Results Not Demonstrated
Department of Agriculture	National School Lunch	Results Not Demonstrated
Department of Agriculture	Natural Resources Conservation Service: National Resources Inventory	Results Not Demonstrated
Department of Agriculture	Resource Conservation and Development	Results Not Demonstrated
Department of Agriculture	Rural Business Enterprise Grant Program	Results Not Demonstrated
Department of Agriculture	Rural Business-Cooperative Service Value-Added Producer Grants	Results Not Demonstrated
Department of Agriculture	Rural Distance Learning and Telemedicine Loan and Grant Program	Results Not Demonstrated
Department of Agriculture	The Emergency Food Assistance Program (TEFAP)	Results Not Demonstrated
Department of Agriculture	USDA Wildland Fire Management	Results Not Demonstrated
Department of Agriculture	Wildlife Habitat Incentives Program	Results Not Demonstrated
Department of Commerce	Coastal Zone Management Act Programs	Results Not Demonstrated
Department of Commerce	Commerce Small Business Innovation Research Program	Results Not Demonstrated
Department of Commerce	International Trade Administration:	Results Not Demonstrated

When developing a sales pipeline, it is very important to include opportunities from the PART ratings. *Think about this*—you are pursuing an opportunity to join a large prime contractor's team. Check out the ExpectMore Web site and look up the program you are researching. This site can give you valuable information in helping you make a decision if you should prime a deal or join a team as a sub. If the program is not doing well, then you know the incumbent contractor is not a good team to be on. You should look for a team to join that offers a solution different than the one with a bad PART rating.

When I help clients develop their sales pipeline, I usually find several programs with lots of funding and low ratings. The goal is to find problems your company can fix. If a federal executive's program is not doing well, then generally that person is open to some new ideas that could improve their program.

Fed Biz Opps (FBO)

Another place to research an agency is the Fed Biz Opps (FBO) database. Their database can be found at *https://www.fbo.gov/.* There are also some very good subscription databases that your company can pay a fee to access, like Input, Fed Sources, Eagle Eye, and epipeline. Many agencies will post their procurement forecasts on their Web sites. DHS does a great job of this. Just remember, subscription databases generally tell us about existing public sector contracts that may or may not come up for recompete. Remember, the key piece of information when you get procurement data from the FBO, subscription databases, or a SADBU forecast is funding—make sure the deal has funding.

I have seen people get fired for chasing a deal that does not have funding or a deal with delayed funding. Pick up the phone and ask the contracting officer if this deal has been funded. If the answer is no, then find something else to chase. The FBO Web site has a very user-friendly search engine. It can be used to learn about upcoming deals and Sources Sought Announcements (SSA). The SSA occurs when the government asks industry for advice about certain technologies. Take a look at what procurements are going on with your customers. Add these opportunities to the sales pipeline.

A great thing about FBO is their e-mail notice feature that sends you e-mail notices on deals you are researching so you do not have to constantly monitor the site for updates. When I begin working with a client on an agency, I frequently spend a day looking at the FBO Web site to get a handle on what has been happening in the agency for the past year. Once I figure out what deals my client is interested in, I will register to receive an e-mail notification whenever the government issues any changes to this procurement.

When using the FBO Web site, click on the Fed Biz Opps Vendors link. After clicking the link, you will see a list of federal agencies letting you choose an agency to review.

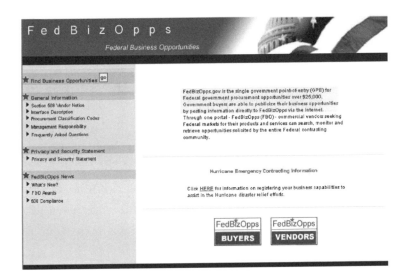

Once you choose the agency you want, look at the procurement activity that has been taking place. The example below shows a search I did for Computer Information Systems at DHS.

Feb 26, 2007
Agency: Department of Homeland Security
Office: Citizenship & Immigration Services
Location: Burlington Administrative Center
➡**Posted:** Feb 26, 2007 **Type:** Amendment 01 **Title:** D -- Telecomm/PBX Lease @ L'Enfant Plaza **SOL:** HSSCCG-0
00026
➡**Posted:** Feb 26, 2007 **Type:** Amendment 03 **Title:** U -- Executive Education **SOL:** HSSCCG-07-R-00003

Feb 23, 2007
Agency: Department of Homeland Security
Office: Citizenship & Immigration Services
Location: Burlington Administrative Center
➡**Posted:** Feb 23, 2007 **Type:** Amendment 05 **Title:** R -- Service Center Operations Support Services **SOL:** HSSC
00002

Office of the Inspector General and the Government Accountability Office

This area of research is very critical and important to your sales pipeline. Let's take a look at Office of the Inspector General (OIG) and the Government Accountability Office (GAO). The President uses the OIG and GAO to keep an eye on the big federal agencies, the ones with lots of funding and power. As you begin to develop your sales pipeline, I encourage looking at both agencies' Web sites. Each department has their own OIG Web site. For example, if you were researching the Department of Commerce, you should look at *http://www.oig.doc.gov/* and *http://www.gao.gov/*, respectively. Also, each agency will have its own internal OIG office. I recommend conducting searches on each agency you are marketing your solution to.

Allow me to give you an example. If you are marketing to the Department of Education, I recommend doing a search on the GAO Web site for *Department of Education* and any keywords that connect with what your company is selling. If you sell Service Oriented Architecture (SOA) solutions, you may want to do a search using the words, *Department, Education,* and *SOA,* so you can quickly learn if the government has any problems they need immediate help solving. In the past, I have helped clients win new business by finding a problem to solve through the GAO or OIG. Here is what the GAO Web site looks like:

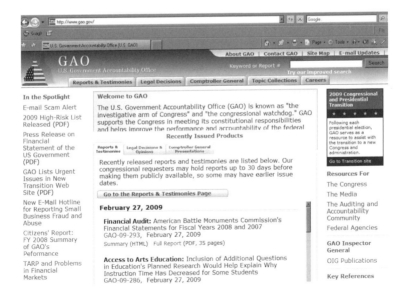

Normally, you can find a handful of problems the government needs help with by looking through the reports on the GAO and OIG Web sites. Remember, after identifying the problem, you need to find the person who owns the problem and talk to that person about how you can help solve his or her issues. Many of the issues in these reports can be addressed by giving the government an unsolicited proposal from your company.

In my career, I have helped clients close deals by finding a problem in the GAO or OIG, and helping the government solve their problems. Here is a sample of what the DHS OIG Web site looks like.

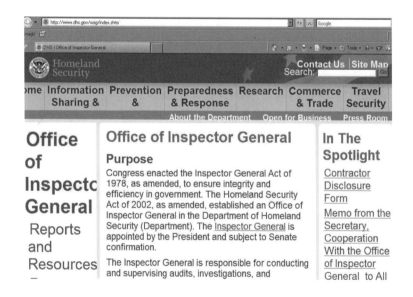

Federal Procurement Data System (FPDS)

The Federal Procurement Data System (FPDS) tells us what Product Service Codes and North American Industry Classification System codes each agency buys from and from whom they buy them. I am not an expert on how the FPDS works. Normally, I just pick up the phone and get a customer service representative to help out, (703) 390-5360, or send an e-mail to them at: *fpdssupport@gce2000.com*. I also recommend using a service like Eagle Eye. This is a terrific tool that can tell you just about anything you need to know about how the government buys.

The following graphic is a screenshot of the FPDS Web site. Whenever I am chasing a deal, I like to get a feel for what companies have contracts with the specific agency as well as how much the government is spending on these folks. Remember, whether you are selling computers, software, or engineering services, the FPDS is a tremendous place to look for information. Let's say you sell hardware and you want to learn the location of your competitors' installed bases. The FPDS can help you get a list of where your competitor has sold its hardware over the last several years. It is truly amazing what can be learned by spending a day with the FPDS.

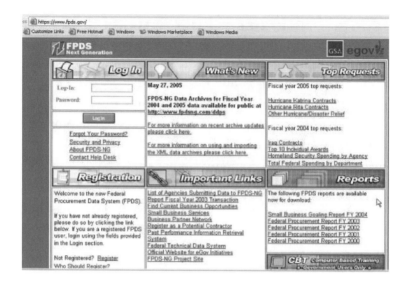

President Bush Created a Web Site in 2007 to Help You Track Federal Spending

Another great source to monitor government spending, contracts, and your potential competition in a government department is *http://www.usaspending.gov/*. This site was created by the *Federal Funding Accountability and Transparency Act of 2006*, which requires full disclosure to the public about organizations receiving federal funding.

According to Public Law 109-182, the Web site will provide the following:

(A) *the name of the entity receiving the award;*

(B) *the amount of the award;*

(C) *information on the award including transaction type, funding agency, the North American Industry*

Classification System code or Catalog of Federal Domestic Assistance number (where applicable), program source, and an award title descriptive of the purpose of each funding action;

(D) the location of the entity receiving the award and the primary location of performance under the award, including the city, State, congressional district, and country;"

(E) a unique identifier of the entity receiving the award and of the parent entity of the recipient, should the entity be owned by another entity; and

(F) any other relevant information specified by the Office of Management and Budget.

Welcome to USASpending.gov - Where Americans Can See Where Their Money Goes

Have you ever wanted to find more information on government spending? Have you ever wondered where federal contracting dollars and grant awards go? Or perhaps you would just like to know, as a citizen, what the government is really doing with your money. The Federal Funding Accountability and Transparency Act of 2006 (Transparency Act) requires a single searchable website, accessible by the public for free that includes for each Federal award:

1. The name of the entity receiving the award;
2. The amount of the award;
3. Information on the award including transaction type, funding agency, etc;
4. The location of the entity receiving the award;
5. A unique identifier of the entity receiving the award.

Welcome to www.USAspending.gov, a relaunch of www.FederalSpending.gov, that provides citizens with easy access to government contract, grant and other award data.

To begin searching, select either the Assistance or Contracts tab at the top left side of this page. You can easily switch back and forth as you search.

The table below provides a summary of the federal spending information available on USASpending.gov. For an overview of the data available on this website, please see the Data Quality tab at the top of this page.

Contracts and Other Spending in Billions of Dollars

As you begin to research opportunities that best match your technology solution, I recommend getting a handle on your competition. One of the great features of this site is the ability to search for specific contractors. For example, let's say I am competing against company XYZ. I can do a search and learn the following about the company:

- How much money in government contracts this company has received in specific fiscal years

- Number of contracts this company has and transactions

- Top 5 Congressional Districts where their contract work is performed

- Top 5 agencies that purchase from this company

- Top 5 products/services sold by this company to the government

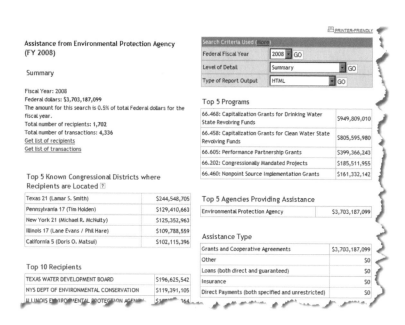

As you go into new departments and agencies to look for business, it is very important to know who your competition is and what they are selling.

The other feature I want to point out on this site is, you have the search ability to look at subcontracts in your targeted agency. This will be a very useful tool when you are comparing your team going after a bid to the incumbent team that currently has the contract. Later in the book, we discuss the difference between going after business as a prime or sub.

The last point I want to make about this site is that it also provides you a good snapshot of an agency's spending and top contracts, as shown in the previous diagram.

The Press

Our last research tool is the press. Find out what magazines or blogs the customer is reading. What industry publications report on your target customer? Each day in my Inbox, I receive a minimum of 3 to 5 newsletters telling me something about the federal government and how it buys. When I am starting to research an agency for a client, I read all the press articles over the past year concerning the agency to find out what their key issues are, which executives are coming and going, what companies are doing well, which ones are not, and what opportunities in that agency are making the headlines. Here is a list of my favorite Web sites I use to learn about my federal customers:

http://www.acq.osd.mil/dpap/sitemap.html

http://www.afji.com

http://www.aviationnow.com

http://www.cq.com

https://www.epls.gov/

http://www.fcw.com

http://www.federaltimes.com

http://fedscoop.com/

http://www.gcn.com

http://www.gfoa.org

http://www.google.com/unclesam

http://www.governmentbusinessbook.biz

http://www.governmententerprise.com

http://www.govexec.com

http://www.govloop.com

http://www.govpro.com

http://www.govtech.net

http://www.govwest.com

http://www.homelanddefensejournal.com

http://www.hppmag.com

http://www.hstoday.us

http://www.info.gov/phone.htm#independent

http://www.jamesjbaker.com

http://www.mit-kmi.com

http://www.ndia.org

http://www.public-cio.com

http://www.sba.gov

http://www.thehill.com

http://www.toolsandtactics.com

http://www.washingtontechnology.com

http://www.washingtonpost.com

Also, take a look at the agency's Web site. I recommend going out to *http://www.usa.gov*. They provide a great index that literally takes you right to the agency's Web site.

The world is changing very fast. Social media and Web 2.0 are changing the way we communicate and receive information. Over the last few years, there has been a trend where an employee and/or senior decision-maker of a company or agency will literally post a blog of their thoughts as it relates to that organization. I encourage reading some of the federal blogs for information. Remember, we are looking for business problems to solve. Below are some of the blogs I look at:

The Briefing Room—Blog
http://www.whitehouse.gov/blog

Evolution of Security—TSA Blog
http://www.tsa.gov/blog

Fast Lane—U.S. Department of Transportation
http://fastlane.dot.gov/

Future Digital System Blog—U.S. Printing Office
http://fdsys.blogspot.com/

GovGab—General Service Administration
http://blog.usa.gov/roller/govgab/

Military Health System Blog
http://www.health.mil/mhsblog/

NASA Goddard CIO Blog
http://blogs.nasa.gov/cm/blog/Goddard%20CIO%20Blog

Pushing Back Blog—National Drug Control Policy
http://pushingback.com/blogs/pushing_back/default.aspx

Walter Reed Health Care System Commander's Blog
http://blogs.wramc.amedd.army.mil/Hospital/default.aspx

Health and Human Services
http://secretarysblog.hhs.gov

Congressional Budget Office
http://cboblog.cbo.gov

Greenversations—Environmental Protection Agency
http://blog.epa.gov/blog/

DHS Leadership Blog
http://www.dhs.gov/journal/leadership/

Navy
http://www.doncio.navy.mil/Blog.aspx

Library of Congress
http://www.loc.gov/blog/

DipNote—State Department's Public Blog
http://blogs.state.gov

By the time this book is in print, I am sure many other federal blogs will be out there. A complete listing of all current and past government blogs is available at: *http://www.usa.gov/Topics/Reference_Shelf/News/blog.shtml.*

After reading all the press articles, blogs, and agency Web sites, make a list of a few stories that discuss problems the government needs help solving, and add them to your sales pipeline as potential opportunities.

Wrap Up

Before we move on from research and discuss how we take all this information and create a sales pipeline, lets do a quick review of what we covered:

1. Write down what your business does using keywords

2. Do keyword search on the OMB budget Web site to look for funded information technology opportunities (note DME versus Steady State)

3. Look at targeted agencies' small business forecast and strategy plans

4. FOIA or contact agency to get copy of their 300's

5. Review the PART for targeted agencies (look for solutions and improvements your firm can make)

6. Look in FedBiz for RFIs or new opportunities in your targeted agencies

7. Go to targeted GAO and agency's OIG site and conduct a keyword search to look for problems you may be able to fix

8. Use the press and blogs to learn more about the customer and other problems you may be able to fix

9. Place all opportunities in an Excel spreadsheet and assign a value to them to identify those deals that best match your company's offerings

Chapter 2

Building Your Sales Pipeline

What Now?

Now that we have gathered all this research, the question is, what should we do with it? The next step is to weigh all the information we have collected. We have hundreds of pieces of information, ranging from the Information Technology (IT) budget and business cases, to announced deals and press articles. We cannot possibly chase all this business. Therefore, we have to figure out a way to take this research and turn it into actionable items that may result in business for your company. As we develop our criteria, here are some key areas to think about:

- Do we have solutions to fix the problem?

- Do we have past performance in the agency?

- Do we need other partners to chase this deal?

- Do we have time to really chase this deal?

- What are our next steps?

Scoring Deals

Remember, this is subjective—you can pick numbers and factors that work for you. I usually pick a set of numbers that will add up to 20. If a deal gets 15 to 20 points, it is a priority 1 opportunity that I should spend much of my time and energy pursuing. If a deal gets 4 points, it is something not worth my time. Normally, I will score a deal based on timing, technical qualifications, past performance, agency knowledge, and the value of the deal.

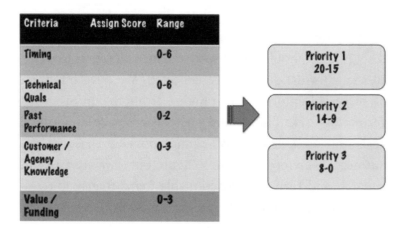

Criteria	Assign Score	Range
Timing		0-6
Technical Quals		0-6
Past Performance		0-2
Customer / Agency Knowledge		0-3
Value / Funding		0-3

Priority 1
20-15

Priority 2
14-9

Priority 3
8-0

Let's spend a moment breaking down each of the areas. Remember, we may not be able to assess all the information of a deal at first glance. If this is the case, then make a hypothesis or do more research to determine whether or not the deal can truly be worked. Okay, let's get started. Go gather all our research so we can figure out what you can chase or put in good old File 86 aka your trash can. We will look at each business case, announced deal, budget line item, and press article to assess the following:

Timing. Many federal deals can take 6 to 18 months to close. The big boys are looking at deals usually a year or more in advanced. As you get closer to the RFP date, the more difficult an opportunity becomes to pursue. It is my opinion that the government usually enters into a "blackout period" two months or so before an RFP hits. During this "blackout period" the government will not speak with industry. The other key question to think about is whether you have time to meet with the senior decision-makers and demonstrate your unique selling proposition. Many agencies have an Investment Review Board (IRB) that will examine all technical solutions. It is probably not a bad idea to meet with as many folks as possible that are on the IRB.

Technical qualifications. Can your company really do the work that is required? Do you have any gaps or cracks in your solution? Take time to look at this because I guarantee your competition will.

Past performance. Where have you done this before? In years past, the government was more interested in federal past performance. Today, the government will look at commercial past performance. The government is very interested in industry best standards.

Agency knowledge. This is one of the biggest problems for many companies. They do not take time to know the agency's goals, lines of business (LOBs), organization, decision-makers, and key issues.

Value. Is this deal big enough or small enough for you to go after? If you are a ten-person company, then chances are a $100 million deal is too big for you to prime. But a deal that is $1 million may be more in line with what you can truly handle. Also, can you competitively price your offerings to win?

Creating Your Pipeline

After we weigh and score all the information gathered in Chapter 1, Research, it is time to put this data down in writing. There are all kinds of sales tracking tools available. I tend to stick with a basic Microsoft Excel spreadsheet, putting the opportunities in order by priority number. The following is an example of a method I have used for the past ten years.

Opp	Priority Level	Description	Value	Value to Your Company	Timing	Your Firm's Value to Deal	Agency Past Performance	Next Steps
1	Insert ranking	Insert summary of what the agency is trying to do	Insert budget number	Based on your company's solution you provide to the deal, make a guess of what your value would be ($500K)	When is the RFP	List of your firm's value to deal: Security Mgmt Web	What agency past performance do you have or list commercial or like performance	Make call plan

Let's take a few moments to review each part of the spreadsheet. Remember, add or delete columns in order to mirror the spreadsheet to your company's specific requirements.

Priority level. Deals that scored the highest should be put first. This is where you want to spend most of your time.

Description. Simply state the issue that needs to be fixed. The government wants to buy XYZ to fix ABC or the Government Accountability Office (GAO) report said the government needs more help with ABC because they have a problem with XYZ.

Value. How much could the deal be worth if you win? It is easy to tell this if there is an existing contract or budget line item. However, when reading a report, press article, or other data that does not have a number, remember your seventh grade science class and make a hypothesis or educated guess. Think to yourself, "How much would it cost us to fix this problem based on what we know?" Again, this is an estimate, as you research the deal in more depth, you may need to change this number.

Value to your company. Does your company offer products and services that only fix half of the problem? Take a $1 million deal: If you can only do half of the work, then this opportunity is only worth $500,000 to you. Here's another example: Let's say you are a hardware company that sells servers. You read an article that says the government is going to buy a new procurement system. Next, you read the RFP and realize that although the total program is $400 million, this opportunity requires 40 to 50 servers, which may mean your real value is $500,000.

Your firm's value to customer. What is unique about how your company can solve the government's problem? Why are you better than your competitors? What does the government customer say about your product or service? Always know your value to a deal.

Past performance. Insert past performance specific to that agency. Tell the government where else you have worked in their department, command, directorate, or commercial reference that has a similar size and scope to their requirements.

Next Steps

Now that we know an opportunity is worth pursuing, we need to develop a call plan. Take a look at an agency's organization chart, IRB, and other points of contact from the business case. Literally, make a list including names, titles, organizations, e-mails, phone numbers, and roles with the procurement. I will go into more detail about how to make a call plan and cold-calling in Chapter 5, Communicating Your Value Proposition.

In the meantime, go through all your research, weigh the information, and upload it into a spreadsheet. This is an exercise that all senior business development, marketing, and sales executives should do.

Chapter 3

The Deal

When I first started in federal sales back in the early 1990s, I quickly learned that all deals have 3 parts: contracts, partners/teaming, and government demand creation. In order to win a deal, you will have to provide a strategy for the government client consisting of the contract type and partners your customer likes to use.*

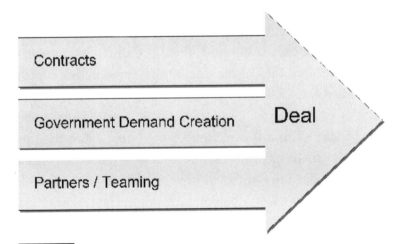

---

* Visit my Web site, *http://www.toolsandtactics.com/*, for a CD that can assist with the entire capture process.

Contracts

All agencies use contracts to purchase their required needs. In current-day federal procurement, more and more deals go through the General Service Administration (GSA), Schedule 70, and Government-wide Acquisition Contracts (GWACs) than they do open competition. The reason why federal procurement is moving to the GWAC process is because it makes buying easier for each agency. Think about this from an administrative standpoint. By standardizing all federal purchases and having them go through one vehicle, there is no need to create individual procurements for each requirement.

The tough thing about GWACs and GSA schedules is that the day the contract is awarded, you get a big, fat zero in revenue. These are contracts the agency will use to buy something—it is not a guarantee for millions of dollars to your company, but a right to market your contract to that agency. With that being said, there are different numbers floating around the Washington, D.C. Capital Beltway. Each year, there are billions of dollars that go through the GSA for the purchase of IT services and products. During the time I was writing this section of the book, I had the opportunity to speak with a senior official at DHS, and trust me with what I am about to say, this official said the bulk of their purchases will be going through EAGLE and First Source GWACs. *Have GWACs on your pipeline but remember they are only a license to hunt.*

Here are some key issues to think about when pursuing an opportunity:

- Do you need a contract vehicle to sell to your federal customer?
- What vehicle does your prospect use to buy?
- Do you have this vehicle?
- How can you gain access to the vehicle?
- Always be ready to give an unsolicited proposal

Just a quick note on unsolicited proposals

Over the years, I have seen many companies figure out a way to solve a government problem. Allow me to get technical for a moment. Take the time necessary to become familiar with Federal Acquisition Regulation (FAR). I was very fortunate in the early 1990s to literally go to FAR school. The company I worked for at the time paid for a master's certificate program in federal procurement at George Washington University in Washington, D.C. I went to a week-long class and studied FAR. You may read about FAR at: *http://www.arnet.gov/far/*. I definitely recommend studying FAR 15.603c. This regulation states what an unsolicited proposal must be:

(c) A valid unsolicited proposal must—

> *(1) Be innovative and unique;*

> *(2) Be independently originated and developed by the offeror;*

(3) *Be prepared without Government supervision, endorsement, direction, or direct Government involvement;*

(4) *Include sufficient detail to permit a determination that Government support could be worthwhile and the proposed work could benefit the agency's research and development or other mission responsibilities;*

(5) *Not be an advance proposal for a known agency requirement that can be acquired by competitive methods; and*

(6) *Not address a previously published agency requirement.*

Remember, look for a problem to solve and simply offer the solution. There is no better way to create demand. Take a look at the following Web site: *http://www.acquisition.gov/far/current/html/FARTOCP15 .html.*

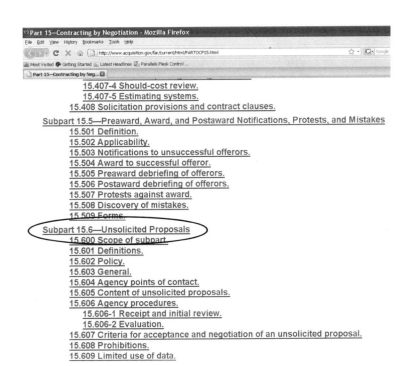

On the Web site above, click on the part that says, Subpart 15.6 - Unsolicited Proposals. I don't think I could have said it better myself. Let's review:

15.605 Content of unsolicited proposals.

Unsolicited proposals should contain the following information to permit consideration in an objective and timely manner:

(a) Basic information including—

(1) Offeror's name and address and type of organization; e.g., profit, nonprofit, educational, small business;

(2) Names and telephone numbers of technical and business personnel to be contacted for evaluation or negotiation purposes;

(3) Identification of proprietary data to be used only for evaluation purposes;

(4) Names of other Federal, State, or local agencies or parties receiving the proposal or funding the proposed effort;

(5) Date of submission; and

(6) Signature of a person authorized to represent and contractually obligate the offeror.

(b) Technical information including—

(1) Concise title and abstract (approximately 200 words) of the proposed effort;

(2) A reasonably complete discussion stating the objectives of the effort or activity, the method of approach and extent of effort to be employed, the nature and extent of the anticipated results, and the manner in which the work will help to support accomplishment of the agency's mission;

(3) Names and biographical information on the offeror's key personnel who would be involved, including alternates; and

(4) Type of support needed from the agency; e.g., facilities, equipment, materials, or personnel resources.

(c) Supporting information including—

(1) Proposed price or total estimated cost for the effort in sufficient detail for meaningful evaluation;

(2) Period of time for which the proposal is valid (a 6-month minimum is suggested);

(3) Type of contract preferred;

(4) Proposed duration of effort;

(5) Brief description of the organization, previous experience, relevant past performance, and facilities to be used;

(6) Other statements, if applicable, about organizational conflicts of interest, security clearances, and environmental impacts; and

(7) The names and telephone numbers of agency technical or other agency points of contact already contacted regarding the proposal.

Many agencies will provide advice on their Web sites about how to present an unsolicited proposal. Here is an example from a DHS Web site:

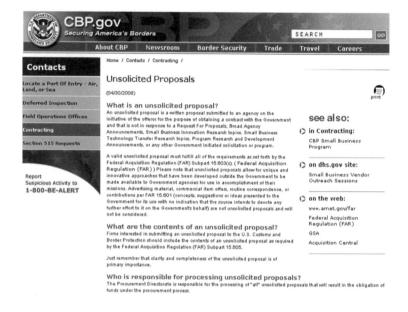

Take the time to prepare an unsolicited proposal. The government has an obligation to meet with you and review your proposal.

Partners / Teaming

This year the federal budget is around $70 billion. By now, we have gone on the Office of Management and Budget (OMB) Web site and took a look at the federal IT forecast. My *unofficial opinion* is that at least 70 percent of federal business goes through the channel/integrator community. My goal is not to debate the percentage, but to point out that a whole lot of dollars float through some pretty big three- and four-letter acronym companies. If you drive down the Dulles Toll Road in Virginia, you can see many of these companies' signs from the interstate.

The first thing we need to figure out is whether you are going to be the prime or sub. Both sides of the coin have their advantages and disadvantages. Generally, my advice to clients is to always be the prime on a deal when possible. The government will look at the size of your company and its revenues to determine if it is a risk doing business with you—i.e. does your company have enough stability that the government can trust your organization to administer a program/technical solution.

If you happen to be a sub, always pick the team that has the highest probability to win. When I first began this business back in the early '90s, I really did not think this way. Instead I thought, "If I could just get on one of the *big players'* teams, I would have a chance." One of the first things I learned is there are only one or two companies that really have a chance at winning a competitive proposal. GWACs are a very different story. Go and look at each prime as hard as they are looking at you. Before meeting with potential primes, spend some time talking with the government customer to create demand for what your company offers. I recommend doing the following before meeting with potential primes:

1. Locate the end user. Go to the agency's Web site and see if you can get an organization chart. I also recommend using paid subscription services, resources like Carroll's Publishing and Leadership Directories. Try to find the Chief Information

Officer (CIO), Chief Financial Officer (CFO),
Program Manager (PM), and other technical people
involved in the procurement. Also, many agencies
will post who is on their Information Review Board
(IRB). This is another great place to talk to people
about government issues.

2. Go to the Federal Procurement Data System
(FPDS) and see who is doing business in that
agency. You may also want to subscribe to a service
like Eagle Eye.

3. Go to a subscription database like Input,
epipeline, or FedSources and do a search under
awards to see what companies have won recent
deals in that agency.

4. Take those prime contractor names you get from 1,
2, and 3 and do a quick search in the press and
Government Accountability Office (GAO). Make
sure no one has any bad press. Trust me, the
government will find out if your prime has any
skeletons in its closet.

5. There are several pricing experts around the Capital
Beltway. Understanding how your competition and
teaming partners will price is essential to your
company's survival and growth. There are all kinds
of tricks and techniques to price a proposal. I am
not a pricing expert but recommend using the
Freedom of Information Act (FOIA) to look at a
company's past contract. Also, take a glance at

their published GSA rates and their EDGAR listing at: *http://www.sec.gov/edgar/quickedgar.htm*. One of the most interesting exercises I have learned over the years is how to predict a competitor's pricing range for a deal by looking at their 10K reports.

6. Read the proposal very carefully. I usually look at section K, L, and M. For more information on Proposal Sections K, L, and M, refer to the acronym glossary.

7. Make a chart like below and insert all the evaluation factors:

Prime Contractor	Eval. Criteria: Past Performance (1–25 points)	Eval Criteria: Relationship with Agency (1–25 points)	Eval Criteria: Technical Skills (1–25 points)	Other Data Not Listed in the Bid (1–25 points)
Company 1				
Company 2				
Company 3				
Company 4				
Company 5				
TOTALS –				

8. Go and talk to the primes and fill out the chart. Remember, primes only care if you can bring the cost of their proposal down or add some unique technical discriminator they cannot provide to the customer.

After completing this exercise, the numbers always lead to the top one or two teams.

Approaching the Prime Contractor

When calling a prime, it is very important to meet with their customer first. Next, you must know your value proposition. *Please, please don't send a blanket e-mail to every prime chasing the deal.* Take a few minutes to leave someone a message and then follow it up with an e-mail agenda. I delete countless e-mails from companies telling me about what they do. In the Chapter 5, Communicating Your Value Proposition, we will discuss specific techniques to communicate with prime contractors and the government end user. In the following chapter, we will discuss demand creation strategies.

Chapter 4

Creating Government Demand

Many people confuse sales, business development, marketing, and branding. This is not a how-to-market-and-brand book. However, I do want to spend a few moments discussing some important aspects of these business functions and how each of these functions results in new business for your company.

Sales and Business Development

The goal of selling is to identify the right people that will buy your service or products. I have spent a good part of my career as a sales person with a sales quota. My goal was to sell a certain dollar amount of products and/or services over a 3 to 6 month period. If I made those goals, then I was financially rewarded.

A business development executive is a person that generally chases business opportunities that cannot be closed in a 3 to 6 month window. If you go to an online job search engine and search for business development positions in the Washington, D.C. market, lots of business development job listings will appear because of the long time frame it takes to close a federal deal. Typically, a deal in the federal government can take someone 12 to 24 months to chase. A business developer will strategically work to understand the customer's issues and strategically align his or her company with the best team possible to capture the win for his or her company. I have been blessed to learn my business development skills from some of the best business developers in the game. Remember, a business developer will use some of the skills of a sales and marketing person combined with a strategic understanding of the customer's business issues. I am currently working on a CD series called *Tools and Tactics* that will delve more into the business development and capture aspects of federal business. For more information concerning *Tools and Tactics*, please refer to this Web site: *http://www.toolsandtactics.com/*.

Marketing

Marketing creates an awareness that ultimately creates a sales lead. Yes, it is that simple but be careful where you spend your marketing time and money. When I was the director of business development for a start-up 8(a) firm in Dulles, Virginia, I was constantly getting invited to government marketing events designed to teach people how to market to the government. These events promised people from the government and the big integrators would be there. However, many of these events were simply a waste of time. You have to really ask yourself, "Will my target market, the people who have decision authority to buy my stuff, really be at this event?" If the answer is no, then do not go. If the answer is yes, then go to the event with the purpose of engaging that person and learning something about his or her business problems.

The Industry Advisory Council (IAC) is a great organization to join. They have several shared interest groups (SIG) where a person can go and learn about an agency's problems. I remember years ago, when I was working on an account for a provider of Radio Frequency Identification (RFID) solutions, I needed to get up to speed on what RFID was and why the government needed RFID. At the time, IAC had a Homeland Security SIG. I was able to go once a month and hear from government folks in Homeland Security about their challenges and issues. Imagine the impact this had on my campaign. IAC is reasonable to join and you can learn more about them at: *http://www.iaconline.org/*.

As a consultant to technology companies, I spend a great deal of time researching their target market's key technology issues. After gathering research, I create a way to communicate with their target audience that indicates we understand the target audience's biggest challenges. Sometimes, it is only one piece of direct mail, other times, it is a large campaign spanning over a year.

Branding

The process of creating an image or logo that creates an awareness of your product or service to a specific demographic is called branding. Two years ago, I was in the market to buy my son a new video game system. Microsoft did a great job branding their Xbox 360. After watching many of their commercials and talking to my friends, I decided Xbox was the system for my son. Microsoft was not going to send an Xbox salesperson to my door to convince me to buy the product. Instead, they used branding and marketing to notify me about their product.

After doing a lot of price comparison on who had the best pricing for a Xbox 360, I decided that no matter where I went, the system was evenly priced. Right before the Christmas holiday that year, Target developed a direct mailing campaign to all their credit card holders. This campaign offered 10 percent off all Christmas shopping if I came to their store during a certain time period. My mind was set; I would go to Target for the additional 10 percent off my Xbox.

Let me drive home this point with one more example of branding. By the time you read this book, you will most likely have seen Microsoft's commercials with the tagline, "I'm a PC." These are great commercials designed to change the perception of a personal computer (PC) from the damage done by the Apple campaign carried out over the last few years.

I recently purchased my first iMac from Apple this summer. Like many people, I really enjoyed their PC and Mac commercials. Through a variety of advertisements and commercials, Apple made the point that their machine would give me less problems than the PC. Even though I have owned PCs since the 1990s, Apple had effectively branded the idea that they have less problems than a PC based operating system. When it came time to buy my family's new computer, I decided to go with Apple. Apple never needed a sales person or business developer to call me for a year to make the sale. They used some great commercials to get my attention, which ultimately resulted in the sale of a new iMac to the Baker household.

Where People Get Informed

Not all marketing is that simple. The more complex the product, the harder it is to communicate its value. Just remember to identify the target market, their key issues, and how they get informed about the products they need to buy for their agencies. For example, if your company is chasing a major deal in the government with a 20-page proposal limit, figuring out ways outside of the proposal to market your value proposition is essential. Years ago, I was involved in a deal with a big three-letter agency. The team that ultimately won this deal was a small business with the backing of three big acronym partners. Realizing their response to the proposal would not allow them a chance to adequately respond, these companies, prior to the release of the Request for Proposals (RFP), developed a series of brown-bag technology demonstrations and whitepapers that provided the government extensive detail about their solution. They used marketing like Xbox, Microsoft, and Apple to brand and position their solution.

We all live in a time where many smart firms are using video, Web, and podcasts as well as blogs to market goods and services. I recommend reading Geoff Livingston's book,

Now is Gone, to learn what is happening in "new media." Marketing of the future will involve the key elements of "old media" such as whitepapers, Web sites, events, seminars, and webinars, wrapped in an easy-to-use package that offers the online viewer a one-to-one communication experience. No matter the marketing budget, smart companies are using "new media" as the great equalizer.

I volunteer some of my time at local schools to teach kids about sales, marketing, and branding. This past spring, I taught a group of middle school students. None of these children had a degree in marketing nor were they worried about corporate politics. I was truly amazed at the brilliance of their marketing ideas. Their notions were direct, simple, and pure. Their campaigns involved using Web sites, videos, and grassroot efforts. It is really important to keep in mind that marketing to the federal government will involve targeting people between the ages of 50 and 70, those who are not accustomed to going to a Web site to find information as well as people in their 20's and 40's, who are used to having segmented information easily accessible and sent directly to them through online social networks like LinkedIn, Facebook and MySpace.

Branding Your Company

When promoting your technology company, branding is important. I recommend having a theme or mission of what your company is really trying to do. Also, make sure your Web site has a clean look and mirrors all communication from your company. Web sites of the future will not be static.

Instead, they will be dynamic and offer the viewer a way to interact with online groups via chatting and Web videos. Traditionally, a Web site provides contact information, history of your company, news and events, products and services, and provides the viewer a way to purchase goods and services. Over the next several years, we will see more blogs, videos, and collaboration groups being created.

A large Web budget is not necessary to create a decent Web site. I use, *http://www.1and1.com/*, for all of my Web sites. I also recommend a couple of really good branding firms in the Washington, D.C. Metro Area, such as Livingston Communication and Phoenix Creative Group. Again, make sure your marketing and branding campaigns are not generic, but specific to the people who need to hear your message.

How to Determine if You Should Participate in a Marketing Outreach Program

I quickly want to discuss trade shows, seminars, and Webcasts. I am a big proponent of customer-facing events, if done properly. In my opinion, your only goal when participating in an event is to create sales leads. *If the event cannot deliver 5 to 20 leads of people interested in your service, do not waste your time.* As a young director of business development, I wasted many hours going to events that promised small businesses access to customers and the "inside track" on deals. After a long day of standing behind a display table, I would get back to my office and go through a stack of business cards only to find out that most people just stopped by my booth to get the free pen or trinket I was handing out.

I also spend a great deal of time, for clients, creating a micro-audience of decision-makers to attend their event. Frequently, I hear marketing professionals say, "The event was great, we had lots of people come." However, size does not equal a good marketing event. As you plan your event, I would recommend using the formula below:

$$\text{ROI} = \frac{\text{Number of Sales Leads Generated at Value XYZ}}{\text{Cost for Event}}$$

Let's say it costs a company $5,000 to put on an event. A qualified lead is valued at $10,000. If the goal is to create ten qualified leads, the event will generate $100,000 in potential leads. This means a 20:1 return on the initial marketing investment. After the event, stay on the leads and then come back and say, "Event XYZ resulted in a new deal with agency ABC."

Also, make sure the event has a way of getting a prospect to self-identify their business challenges and issues. Ask polling questions, offer a gift for filling out a survey, or simply put a resource on the phone after the event by simply calling attendees to find out:

- What are their business issues?
- Do they have funding or a procurement coming up in next 12 months?
- Would they be interested in meeting with your firm?

My last piece of advice about marketing events is to make sure the event is not too sales pitchy. Think about the last time you sat through a sales pitch that had nothing to do with you and your current challenges. The event should always be about the customer and their business challenges. If you do not know your market's challenges and issues, then research them. In Chapter One, Research, we discuss many techniques on how to find out an agency's challenges. No matter how much research I do, I always like to pick up the phone and talk to someone. For many of the clients I deal with, I generally spend two months researching their target market and interviewing members of that market about their issues.

When appropriate, involve the government and industry experts at your events. Quite frequently when creating events for clients, I will have one or two government experts as keynote speakers, and three to five subject matter experts from industry on a specific event. *The key is to make your event an industry briefing and not just another webinar or seminar.*

Chapter 5

Communicating Your Value Proposition

How we approach people is very important. A couple of years ago, I was teaching a seminar at the University of Maryland and was discussing how people communicate with each other. A businessman in the audience told me: "It must be easy for you to get in and see anyone you want because you have a really big rolodex." This statement could not be further from the truth. I know a few people around town, but that will only get you so far. A majority of the time, I am blazing trails in places I have never been before. The government is a huge, huge market. For example, the Department of Defense (DoD) is one of the largest employers in the United States. Each agency is like a Fortune 50 or Fortune 100 company; they are huge companies with many, many people. Trust me, there is no way to know everyone in an agency. Some people make a 30-year career just focusing on Navy SPAWAR or Census. New people are constantly coming and going in all agencies.

Practicing and developing your communication techniques is a must. I am a member of Toastmasters International. I generally try out most of my techniques on the club and get feedback long before I approach a government client. If the last speech course you took was in high school or college, I strongly recommend joining toastmasters. It is a reasonable cost to join and a tremendous wealth of knowledge.

There are several different techniques we can use to communicate with prospective clients via phone or e-mail.

Phone Call / Voice Mail Message. This is a technique I use when first approaching new prospects. Usually after leaving this message and sending an e-mail, I get in contact with my target.

This is James Baker, xxx.xxx.xxxx. I am calling you on behalf of my client _____ to discuss their value proposition to the _____ deal. I would like to e-mail you an agenda for a meeting to discuss their value to your customer and your team. Please give me a courtesy call back at your earliest convenience at xxx.xxx.xxxx.

E-mail.
Dear Sir or Madam:

Per my voice mail message, I would like to set up a time to meet with you to discuss my client's value to your pursuit of the _____ opportunity. Below is an agenda of what we would like to discuss:

1. Introductions
2. The customer (example: Security Team at Department of Treasury)

3. Why we want to talk to you

4. Value Proposition to customer and your team

5. Discussions / next steps

At your convenience, please give me a few dates that will work for us to meet for 30 minutes to _____ (restate the importance of your value to them). Please call me at xxx.xxx.xxxx or e-mail me at *james@jamesjbaker.com* with any questions.

Regards,

James Baker

Next Steps

When going on a call, always have a next step in mind. I have a sign above my desk that says, *"Where am I in the sales process and what are my priorities to move the deal forward?"* In other words, when meeting with people, always have a purpose and plan as to why you are meeting and the outcome you need to happen from that meeting to create a sale. Author Dale Carnegie says there are 5 steps to every sales cycle:

1. Attention

2. Interest

3. Conviction

4. Desire

5. Close

If you have never read the *5 Great Rules of Selling*, I highly recommend reading this as well as Carnegie's *How to Win Friends and Influence People*. Always keep in mind where you are in the sales cycle.

Remember, the goal is to find out where the customer and prime are having pain, and how to relieve their pain. One of the biggest mistakes people make is thinking of the federal government as a single vertical market. The government has over 27 vertical markets. For example, the government is a huge provider of health care. It buys food and clothes. It has huge logistical operations. Always be aware of the vertical line of business you are in and what your return on investment (ROI) is to those you are partnering with and the customer.

My goal in a meeting with a prime is to sign a nondisclosure agreement (NDA). This allows companies to speak in confidence about the procurement. After meeting with the NDA in place, the next goal should be to get a teaming agreement (TA) in place. Sometimes with a technical sale or joining a large team, you have to show the prime how your solution works as well as give them references. If this is your first time dealing with this type of thing, I would suggest using a good lawyer. I know a handful of very good people who specialize in small business law. I refer many people over to Ken Brody of Brody, Dondershine, and David. It will be well worth the time and money having a professional check the NDA and TA from a large prime. I have seen many companies get screwed because they did not do this. Remember, no company is in business to give it to someone else. *Always beware!*

Return on Investment (ROI)

When approaching the government customer, you need to be prepared to deliver a business case on why your company can be of value to the agency. By business case, I simply mean give the government a reason why they should look at what you are selling. Do you save them money, man hours, or improve operational efficiencies? Whatever case you make, always show what the customer's ROI is by going with your product and/or services.

In Chapter One, Research, we discussed why all agencies fill out business cases (Form 300 A) to get funding from Congress. In my line of work, I get to interview and meet with many of our great leaders in government. One of the *biggest complaints* they have about the vendor community is that they truly do not understand their organizations' issues. I remember one particular interview years ago with the Executive Office of the President. I was meeting with one of the key executives to discuss service oriented architecture (SOA), which along with security, is one of the biggest buzzwords in the federal space right now. I was speaking to this person about his current issues and asked if he had a preference of software he would use for SOA. This person looked me straight in the eyes and said he did not give a _____ (you can fill in the blank) what software was used; he was looking for a software company that really understood his problems first, and then second, how they could fix them. The lucky software company that got a contract with this fellow sure wasn't selling software, but solutions to his problems. Understanding the following key ingredients is essential to developing a successful business case:

- The problem or customer's requirements
- The cost associated with this problem
- A solution to the problem
- The cost savings of your solution to the government
- Internal support and sponsorship

Always remember there are three types of ROI: process improvement, man-hour savings, and cost reduction. Make sure the government prospect knows what ROI you are offering.

Death by PowerPoint

Many of us use PowerPoint to present to potential federal customers. I like PowerPoint but am very careful how I use it. I deal with many clients who have a 60 to 100 page presentations. No one in his or her right mind wants to sit through a 60 to 100 page presentation. I generally advise people to present their value in 7 to 10 slides—*no more. I am very serious about this.* Here is the presentation formula I use:

- Slides 1–2 focus on the prospect
- Slides 3–4 review what you think the problem is and gains concurrence from prospect

- Slides 5–10 explain your solution and savings to the customer

This past Memorial Day I was invited by a good friend of mine to help him prepare a client to ask for money from a bunch of venture capitalists. We took a very technical presentation and did two things to it: we made the presentation a lot smaller and we simplified the overall message. Remember, the audience needs to be able to understand what you do and how you will help them. I usually practice technical pitches on my sons, who are in elementary and middle school. If a normal person can't understand the words you are using, then what makes you think your prospect will? Normally, within three days of meeting someone, we only remember if we like the person or not, and maybe a few phrases of their presentation.

Let me drive this truth home a little further. During the time I am writing this section of the book, I am getting ready to list my house with a new realtor. The market in Virginia is tough. My criteria for selecting a realtor is based on personality (can I work with him or her) and marketing approach (tactics he or she will use to promote my house). Anyway, almost two weeks have gone by and what I really remember about each of the realtors I interviewed was whether I liked them and one or two things about their approach. Here are some important areas to keep in consideration:

First impressions. People make over 35 conscious and unconscious opinions about you in less than 14 seconds based on what you visually look like, the sound of your voice, and the words you use.

Retention. What is the most important thing you want your prospect to remember? If you only had one minute to tell them the most important thing about your solution, what would it be?

Summarize often. There is an age old saying that states you should *tell them, tell them again, and tell them what you told them.*

Understand your audience's personality. We are all wired differently, with the ability to see and hear things differently from anyone else in the whole world. Find out how your prospect likes to receive information. People are generally analytical, visual, or kinetic/tactile. Analytical people like lots of facts and data. Visual people, like me, enjoying seeing pictures of what you are talking about. Kinetic/tactile people place a great deal on their emotions, i.e. what they feel and how you make them feel. Analytical people tend to like lots of detail and are process-oriented. Remember, right- and left-brained people think and act differently, too. Know the personality traits of your audience. Generally, a technical personal will be a left-brained, analytical person. Present accordingly!

Common presentation pitfalls. Over the years, I have seen all kinds of presentation pitfalls. I once saw an engineer deliver a whole presentation to the Department of Transportation with his hand down the backside of his pants. At

COMMUNICATING YOUR VALUE PROPOSITION ◆ 93

the end of the presentation, the prospect avoided shaking hands. I wonder why?

Another time, a very pretty woman gave a sales pitch with a little something extra hanging out of her nose. For her entire presentation, most of us were focused on her nose and not her presentation. Lillian Brown wrote a book called, *Your Public Best*. I highly recommend reading this book. I have had the opportunity to personally meet Lillian Brown. She has helped several generations of presidents prepare for their public presentations. Reading her book will give you great insight into how to prepare for a speech.

In general, here are some of the biggest mistakes I have seen:

- **Ahs and ums.** A few years ago, I attended an event with a major software company in Tyson's Corner, Virginia. The senior vice president who spoke was well-dressed and very smart. The problem was she said over thirty *ums* in her speech. It was awful to listen to *um, um, um, um.* The way not to *ah* and *um* is to rehearse exactly what you are going to say. When you are speaking and the brain does not what to say, most people will *ah* and *um.* I suggest stopping for a second to let your brain catch up!

- **Dress appropriately.** I see many women violate this principle, presentation after presentation, with either too much jewelry or revealing clothing. Look in the mirror before you speak and remove anything that is shimmering or shining. Many people will focus on your shiny device rather than you. About two years ago, I had a meeting with a software company. I was presenting some new marketing ideas with a colleague of mine at the time. When we met the woman to whom we were pitching, we had difficulty looking at her due to her blouse being unbuttoned.

For the men, (no, you're not off the hook!) don't over dress for the people you are meeting with. In today's casual work environment, it is very hard to know how to dress. The worst mistake you can make is wearing a 3-piece suit with a designer tie and great cuff links when your prospect's income and position does not allow them to dress similarly. I generally ask, "What is the dress code in your office?" A pair of khaki pants and a basic polo shirt is very appropriate for the majority of meetings I attend. I generally bring one item that will allow me to dress up or down, depending on what a client is wearing. For example, if I am wearing a polo shirt and khakis, then I'll also wear a sports coat. If I walk into a room and everyone is dressed very casual, I simply take my jacket off. However, if everyone is in a suit and tie, I will not feel out of place. It is important to research your prospect/audience and dress accordingly.

- **Talk about yourself.** I see this happen all the time when other companies approach me. They tell me how big they are, who they know, and how great they are. What they forget to tell me is their value proposition and why they are of benefit to me.

I recently had a sales call with a company that sells an e-mail service. The sales rep called me promptly at one o'clock and we got off to a good conversation. This particular rep used to live in a town that I did many years ago. After we exchanged a few more pleasantries about Centreville, Virginia, the rep quickly started on an overview about all the products and services her company offered. I finally stopped this person in the middle of her sentence and asked the rep if she knew what my company did and why I should buy her products.

She was honest and said she had not looked at our site. I took a few minutes to show her what my company did and went on to tell her my business issues. Again, keep in my mind, I did not want to hear a sales pitch on her company, but on how her company could help me. Remember, before you ever approach a company or person, please take some time to find out why this person needs your company's products or services. A random call to someone without knowledge of what they do and why they should buy your product, will generally result in a poor outcome.

Motivation to Buy

Always understand what will cause the customer to buy. Is it price, fear, compassion, relationships, security, career advancement, or perceived value? Use this knowledge to communicate to your client:

- What business problem can you solve for their organization?

- What are the benefits of your product to *them personally* and their *organization overall?*

- How can the benefits be measured?

- Who is your competition?

- Why is your firm better?

If you only had thirty seconds

Let me tell you a quick story about the importance of knowing your client's motivation to buy. Several years ago, I was working with a software company. We had been targeting to get in the newly formed Department of Homeland Security (DHS). After months of targeting a certain chief information officer (CIO) to meet with my client, the CIO agreed. My client was flying in from out of the country, so I tripled checked with the CIO's assistant that the meeting was still on. My client and I decided to meet up an hour before the meeting to go over our strategy one more time before the big meeting. As we were talking, my cell phone rang. I looked down and it was the number of the CIO's assistant. I looked at my client and said, "Excuse me while I take the call." The CIO's assistant said the meeting needed to be postponed.

I was horrified! My client had spent a great deal of time

and money to come see this CIO. Using my most persuasive tactics, I begged, pleaded, and groveled with this assistant to ask her boss to reconsider. I asked the assistant to write down a single sentence on a piece of paper and hand it to her boss. The sentence basically said that we know you have this problem and we can fix it. Please give us five minutes to speak with you. I also told the assistant this client traveled very far to meet with her boss. The nice assistant finally agreed to give my request to her boss and said she would call me back. I am not known for having a soft voice and my client looked at me and said, "Did she cancel?" I said, "Yes, but I have asked them to reconsider and they said they would call back shortly." A few minutes later, my cell phone rang—it was the assistant. She told me the CIO was tripled-booked, but would speak with us if we would wait to see her. As my client and I headed to DHS, I told him that we only had one shot with this CIO and had to make our message brief. We both decided to trash the 10-page PowerPoint presentation we bought with us. As we stood outside of DHS, we rehearsed specifically what my client would say given one minute or less.

The moment arrived and we were ready to go. The CIO warmly greeted us and introduced us to her colleague. She looked at my client and said, "You have a really good consultant working for you." I thanked the CIO for the kind words and said my client had a value to her organization. My client stood up and looked at a map of her network infrastructure on her wall, pointed to a place on the map and said, "Our product will help right here by doing this better, quicker, and faster. We have done this thing for these companies and this is the result they have found."

The CIO appreciated our brevity and knowledge of her situation. After about thirty minutes, we wrapped up the meeting and had a very clear next step in selling this software suite to DHS. Basically, the CIO had a big three-letter acronym company doing the integration. She gave us the name of the lead on the project and said to call them, tell them we met with her, and that she liked the product. My point in telling you this story is that if you have real value to a person, they will make time to listen to you, but be ready because you may only have one shot to make an unforgettable first impression.

Handling Objections

We all hate objections but get used to them. I have never done a sale where there was not an objection. When you get an objection, I recommend the following:

Listen. Understand what the person is saying. Smart people will generally be curious and ask a lot of questions. Respect what the person is asking and never misrepresent the truth. Generally, when I don't know the answer to an objection, I will say to a prospect, "That is a great question you asked and I don't know the answer but I know someone who does. Would it be appropriate to bring my engineers back for a meeting to answer your question?" Most people appreciate sincerity and honesty. They hate the feel of a "slicky-boy used car salesman" who says, "Absolutely, we can do that! I am not sure how, but we can do it."

Dissect. After listening to the objection, you need to get some more information. Is the person objecting for political, economic, or perceived bias to your product? Let me give you an example. Several years ago, after the 9/11 terrorist attacks, I was working with a voice biometric company that had a solution for DHS to basically monitor suspect terrorists using voice recognition software. This company spent a great deal of time thinking about DHS' problems and a workable solution, but there was one problem. As we began to show DHS senior executives this approach, they said it was "too big brother" of an approach and the American public would be against it. In spite of their objections, we showed them they should use this product. However, for political reasons they would not consider a voice biometric to track people. My point here is that you need to find out the root of an objection. Sometimes, it is for a good reason and other times people have inaccurate information or an opinion not based on facts. The goal of a good salesperson is to dissect objections and decide if the person can be moved to buy your products and services.

Remember. The rules of rhetorical analysis before responding to an objection:

- Make a claim responding to the objection
- Show data to prove it
- Warrant or benefit of person going with what you proposed

Get concurrence. Before going forward, literally ask the person, "You had an objection to ABC. My team and I showed you that ABC is not really a factor to the success of this project in the long run. Do you agree we have shown this?" If the person says no, start all over again. *Do not ever try to speed over an objection.* Once you get the person to agree that the objection has been met, move to the next step of the sales process. Also, be aware of the silent objector. As long as I have been selling technology products and services to the feds, techies travel in packs. You may be presenting to a decision-maker who has two or more people in the room with him or her. Before continuing the presentation after an objection, make sure everyone in the room concurs with your statements.

I have seen many salespeople make the mistake of only getting the highest ranking in person in the room to agree with them, underestimating other support folks in the room. Sometimes support staff will not want to look disrespectful or contradictory to a superior in a meeting. Sometimes after the meeting, smart senior decision-makers will say to the people they trust, "What do you think about these people and their product?" At that moment, the silent people in the room hold the outcome to your deal. Make sure you acknowledge these people in the presentation and absolutely make sure you have heard their objections.

Wrap Up

I want to thank you again for reading my book and I hope I have given some insight into how business really works inside the D.C. Capital Beltway. I wish I had a book like this when I started selling into the federal space in the early '90s. Using the process I have described will help you really find out where the money is and give you techniques to speak with the people who hold the purse strings. Usually when I speak to an audience, I take questions throughout the entire presentation as well as the end. Should you have any questions about any of the information in this book, I welcome a dialogue with you to discuss this information in further detail.

Happy Hunting!

James J. Baker, Jr.
http://www.jamesjbaker.com
http://www.governmentbusinessbook.biz

Glossary and Acronym Index

By the time this book is published, there will be several new words and acronyms buzzing around the federal marketplace not listed here. Make sure to visit the book's Web site, *http://www.governmentbusinessbook.biz/*, for new government words and phrases.

When I first started out in federal selling, there was a very popular course called the Terry Kelly class. This class was a two- or three-day seminar covering all the acronyms and definitions currently used in government procurement. As you become more familiar with the public sector market, you will say entire sentences in acronyms. Since you may not have time to go to a class like I did, the following is a list of some of the key acronyms and terms currently used in the land of federal selling.

300's. Form 300 A is what agencies fill out to submit their business cases. When you are looking for an agency's business case, asking for the 300's will alert most people you want the business case.

53's. Budget line items that get funded by Congress

BFE. Budget Formulation and Execution

BY. Budget Year

CCA. *Clinger-Cohen Act*

CFO. Chief Financial Officer

CIO. Chief Information Officer

CM. Case Management

CPIC. Capital Planning Investment Control

CSO. Chief Security Officer

CY. Current Year

DHS. Department of Homeland Security

DME. Development, Modernization, and Enhancement refers to new money that is going into a program.

DoD. Department of Defense

EAGLE. Enterprise Acquisition Gateway for Leading Edge Solutions

E-GOV. Electronic Government

EIEMA. Enterprise Information Environment Mission Area

EPA. Environmental Protection Agency

FAA. Federal Aviation Administration

FAR. Federal Acquisition Regulation

FBO. Federal Business Opportunities (go here to look for deals in any agency).

FHA. Federal Health Architecture

FM. Financial Management

FOIA. *Freedom of Information Act.* Remember you can FOIA contracts, agency information, and even e-mail addresses. Most agencies have a FOIA you can simply cut and paste into an e-mail.

FPDS. Federal Procurement Data System

GAO. Government Accountability Office

GM. Grants Management

GSA. General Service Administration

GWAC. Government-wide Acquisition Contract

HR. Human Resources

HSDN. Homeland Secure Data Network

IRB. Investment Review Board

IRS. Internal Revenue Service

ISS. Information Systems Security

IT. Information Technology

ITI. Information Technology Infrastructure

LOB. Line of Business

NDA. Nondisclosure Agreement

OIG. Office of the Inspector General

OMB. Office of Budget and Management

OSDBU. Office of Small and Disadvantaged Business Utilization

PART. Program Assessment Rating Tool

PM. Program Manager

PY. Past Year

RFI. Request for Information

RFP. Request for Proposal

ROI. Return on Investment

SADBU. Small and Disadvantaged Business Utilization

Section K. Part of proposal where you give representations, certifications, and other statements.

Section L. Part of the proposal that tells your company how to respond to the bid

Section M. Evaluation factors for award

SETA. Systems Engineering and Technical Assistance

SOA. Service Oriented Architecture

SPAWAR. Space and Naval Warfare Systems Command

SSA. Sources Sought Announcement

Steady State. Refers to funding that is already allocated to a program

TA. Teaming Agreement

TSA. Transportation Security Administration

WEB 2.0. The next phase of the World Wide Web or Internet. Web 2.0 generally refers to the technology and software that allows people to collaborate and share information via the Web.

About the Author

James J. Baker is a noted speaker, author, consultant and expert on the public sector technology marketplace. He has spent the bulk of his career in the Washington, D.C. Metropolitan Area consulting for technology companies that sell to government.

Baker has worked with many technology companies, from Fortune 500's to small businesses, such as HP, Intel, VMware, Sybase, McAfee, Verizon and AT&T.

A graduate of the University of Maryland, Baker currently resides in Rocklin, California with his wife and two sons. To learn more about James Baker, please visit *www.jamesjbaker.com*.

TOOLS&TACTICS

Coming Soon ...

A CD seminar & work book on all the
tools and tactics you need to
research, capture, price, and win
business in the Federal Government.

www.toolsandtactics.com